"Derrick Moore has managed to effectively combine well-known biblical stories and his own life experiences to offer encouragement. . . . His inspirational points offer specific advice that is easy to comprehend and will definitely benefit those who read them."

—WALTER M. KIMBROUGH
President, Philander Smith College

"Derrick Moore is a genuine sports hero who shares from his heart how to live a faith-filled, joy-filled life of power and purpose. He is a lifelong friend of mine who not only talks the talk, but walks the walk. *It's Possible!* will impact thousands of lives. Make sure you're one of them!"

—STEVE SHADRACH
Founder, Student Mobilization Ministry
Author, *The Fuel and the Flame*

"Derrick Moore is everyone's wanna-be best friend. His contagious personality comes alive in *It's Possible! Turn Your Dreams into Reality*. Derrick is the real deal—no fluff, no flattery, and no quit. Get to know him and let his secret to success become yours."

—C. PEYTON DAY
President, Day Hospitality Group

"Derrick Moore is a true man of God who brings joy at the mere sight of him and is an inspiration each moment you are with him. In his book, Derrick motivates and inspires us with his great faith and love of God. This is a book you won't want to put down."

—TIM PENDELL
Senior Director of Community Affairs, Detroit Lions

"Derrick Moore's *It's Possible!* is absolutely inspiring! So often we forget just how big of a God we serve, and we give in to discouragement and despair. But Moore reminds us that with God, all things are possible—even the most lofty of goals. It is my prayer that *It's Possible!* would encourage and motivate you to pursue with great passion your God-given dreams and allow Him to make them a reality."

—LES STECKEL
President/CEO, Fellowship of Christian Athletes

"I recommend this book wholeheartedly for anyone who is questioning or struggling to understand God's purpose and direction for his or her life."

—MICHAEL BUNKLEY
Chaplain, Carolina Panthers

IT'S POSSIBLE!

TURN YOUR DREAMS INTO REALITY

DERRICK MOORE

Kregel
Publications

It's Possible! Turn Your Dreams into Reality

Published by Kregel Publications, a division of Kregel, Inc., P.O. Box 2607, Grand Rapids, MI 49501.

This book is designed to inspire the reader and is not intended to be an authoritative source of legal, medical, psychological, or theological information or advice.

Library of Congress Cataloging-in-Publication Data
Moore, Derrick C.
It's possible : turn your dreams into reality / by Derrick Moore.
    p. cm.
1. Dreams—Religious aspects—Christianity. 2. Visions. 3. Success—Religious aspects—Christianity. I. Title.
BR115.D74M66   2008   248.4—dc22   2008006917

ISBN 978-0-8254-3359-7

Printed in the United States of America

08 09 10 11 12 / 5 4 3 2 1

For my mom, Ann Moore, who always taught me that, with God, it's possible. May all readers be so inspired as they venture through this book. Just as I reached my it, your it is attainable as well. Keep believing!

Contents

Acknowledgments

I would like to express my heartfelt passion to every individual who is up against the challenges of life. To those who feel that their dream is only a dream but can never become reality, I want you to know that I have seen dreams become reality—and you can too. The God of the Bible is the One who makes dreams come true. He provides the hope that is necessary to make your dreams possible.

One of my dreams was to see this book become a reality. Here is a special thank you to the people who helped me:

To my wife, Stephanie Perry Moore, who is reaching her *it* daily as she writes novels for God.

To my daughters, Sydni Derek and Sheldyn Ashli, who make Daddy strive to achieve greatness so I can provide for you.

To my new son, Leon Thomas, whom I am honored to father. Keep understanding that I'm tough on you so that you'll one day reach your *it* for God.

And to my extended family—Perrys, Moores, Bruces,

and Roundtrees—your prayers and love help push me to keep making a difference.

To my friends Randy Roberts, Antonio London, Kenneth Perry, Harry Colon, Brett Perriman, Bobby Lundy, Steve Shadrach, Dave Wilson, Tommy Robinson, and Patrick Nix, your unfailing support never fails to recharge me. When I feel I'm worn out or that I'm not making an impact, you pump me back up and help me not to quit.

To the folks I work with: Coach Gailey; Coach Hewitt and the entire Georgia Institute of Technology athletic staff; Fellowship of Christian Athletes; my board members, especially the Stockbridge office staff—Sid, Susan, and Shep; and other chaplains across the NCAA—Chett Williams (Auburn), Wes Yeary (Auburn), Tony Eubanks (Clemson), James Mitchell (Tennessee), Kevin Hines (Georgia), John Rainey (Old Miss), and Danny Buggs (West Virginia). God bless you all.

To my publishing company, Kregel Publications, especially Jim Kregel.

To my assistant, Ciara Roundtree: together I know we'll make a difference for Him.

To all the college athletes I've worked with over the years, especially Calvin Johnson, James Johnson, Michelle Tyree Reese, Chris Reese, Colvin Williams, Brad Brezina, D'Andre Bell, Brandon Duckett, April Johnson, Lance Bowling, Michael Johnson, Michael Matthews, Nate Curry, PJ Daniels, Eric Henderson, Jonathan Cox, and Jewel Welch, thank you for your trust and your love. If you ever need me, know that I'm here.

To every reader of this book, may the truth you find here make a difference.

And to my Lord and Savior, Jesus Christ: it's all about You!

Introduction

*Jesus looked at them and said, "With man this is
impossible, but with God all things are possible."*

MATTHEW 19:26

Everyone has an *it*—a particular hope, a dream, a goal that
they'd like to accomplish, or even a problem or situation
they'd like to see solved. But not everyone knows how to
make their *it* happen. In fact, many people don't believe
their *it* is even *possible*. If you have an *it* that has captured
your attention, and all you can think about is how you can
make *it* happen, don't stop believing.

When the dream seems inconceivable, but you *have* to
achieve it, don't stop believing.

When the resources can't be found, but you need the
money badly, don't stop believing.

When the doctor says there is nothing more to be done,
but you want healing, don't stop believing.

What happens when it seems that all hope is gone? What
do you do when *it* seems impossible?

Don't put down this book. I've got something life-changing to tell you.

We each have an *it* that keep us hoping and dreaming—that one thing that keeps us thinking, *Maybe, just maybe, it could happen.* You know what I'm talking about—that *it* that you always dream about. That *it* that sometimes keeps you awake at night with three of your closest friends—Bloodshot Eyes, Always Yawning, and Bags Under Your Eyes. Sound familiar?

Well, what you're about to discover in the next twelve chapters of this book is that what seems impossible is actually possible.

You can move mountains.

You can cross oceans.

You can survive the storm.

You can achieve your dream and see your *it* become a reality.

Be encouraged. Others have gone before you and blazed the trail.

To achieve greatness in whatever your pursuit is, you need to be motivated, empowered, energized, and inspired. In the Bible, you'll find a road map to greatness, a series of dynamic stories of hope and possibility that will open the way to your *it*.

All the keys for success are already inside your heart and inside God's Word. To know that your *it* can happen, you need to believe in yourself and believe in your dream, but most importantly, you need to believe in God.

I'm writing this book from my own personal experience. When I was growing up, my *it* was larger than life: I wanted to play professional football. Yet I was a poor young man with no apparent resources to reach my dream. All along the way, people told me, "Derrick, you're not fast enough." "Derrick, you're not talented enough." "Derrick, you didn't go to the right school." "Derrick, you can't play in the NFL."

I knew my dream wasn't going to be easy to achieve. I was from a single-parent home. I had very few positive influences in my life, no money, no external motivations, questionable talent, and if you were to ask those who knew my situation, seemingly no hope. All I had was my built-in motivation and my *it*, my dream. Thankfully, that was enough to keep all those negative comments from stopping my belief that *it could happen.*

So, take my word for it: you can't let all the negative things that stand in your way stop you from reaching your goal.

This book is about turning the odds in your favor. I'm not saying that what you're seeking, hoping, and praying for will happen. My goal is to provide you with a mustard seed of hope that, with God, *all things are possible.*

It's possible that you can go from zero to hero. It's possible that every dream you have can be realized. It's possible that you can find sweet relief from the illness that has gripped your life.

It's possible!

Let me say it again: It's possible!

How do I know that?

Because God says it is.

Chapter 1

From Nothing to Something
YOU ALREADY HAVE MORE THAN YOU THINK

Motivational Point

Be very excited! You're on your way! Although you want something big to happen and you have no plan right now for how to change your circumstances, don't be discouraged. You're moving in the right direction—even when everything looks bleak and what you want seems unattainable. Just because you are where you are—no hope, no chance, no way—doesn't mean your predicament will continue. There's light at the end of your dark tunnel. Come on, let's walk toward your *it*.

Let me tell you something right up front: I understand your situation.

No, I may not know your exact circumstances, but I understand your situation.

Right now, you're focused on your nothingness rather than on the somethingness that's out there to be achieved.

And you're frustrated.

But right here, right now, there's an opportunity to chart a new course.

I understand why you might be skeptical that things can turn around. After all, *nothing* means *nothing*—no points on the scoreboard, no food in the cupboard, no gas in the car, and no money in the bank.

We're both aware that nothing is a long way from something. It can be as far as poverty is from prosperity, or chaos is from calm, or evil is from good. But we can't dwell on that. Dwelling on all the things we *don't* have will only hold us back.

Here's a question to ponder: What do you do when you have nothing and something is what you want?

Maybe for you the answer has always been, *Well, I don't know.*

If that's your typical response, it's time to find a new answer.

It's okay if you don't know what to do. But it's not okay if you know what to do and don't do it.

What keeps most people from succeeding isn't what they don't know—it's what they do know and never act on.

Millions of people remain unaccomplished because they've failed to act on what they know and thus have forfeited what they've always hoped for.

What I'm trying to say is really quite simple: You've got to do something in order to get something. And in order to do something, you must first believe in something. The "something" I'm referring to are the promises that are "yes" and "amen" through the person of Jesus Christ (see 2 Cor. 1:17–22). He turns *nothings* into *somethings*. He's been doing it since the beginning, and he will continue to do it until the end (see Rev. 22:13).

Before we move on to the next section, a word of caution

to the impatient ones: If you're in a hurry to make your *it* happen, you need to know that you don't always get from nothing to something overnight. Sometimes it takes a while. The journey can be long and tedious. The road can be rocky and crooked. The obstacles can be challenging and painful. I'm not saying there aren't cases where something can be found suddenly. But in most cases, be prepared for the long haul, and commit yourself to not giving up until you reach your goal.

Take comfort in knowing that anything you take to God has the potential for growing. It could grow into the steps you need to make your dream happen. On the other hand, it might grow into a *delay*, because God wants you to focus on Him until He knows you're ready for your dream to be realized. It might grow into a *no*, because God has something better for you. Either way, in God's hands your *it* is far from nothing. Your *it* has potential.

The fact that you have a dream is something in itself—so, you see, you're not even starting from nothing. Now it's time to take your dream to God and allow Him to tell you what's next. You're on your way to something!

Spiritual Point: Jesus Turns Water into Wine (John 2:1–11)

On the third day a wedding took place at Cana in Galilee. Jesus' mother was there, and Jesus and his disciples had also been invited to the wedding. When the wine was gone, Jesus' mother said to him, "They have no more wine."

"Dear woman, why do you involve me?" Jesus replied. "My time has not yet come."

His mother said to the servants, "Do whatever he tells you."

Nearby stood six stone water jars, the kind used by the Jews for ceremonial washing, each holding from twenty to thirty gallons.

Jesus said to the servants, "Fill the jars with water"; so they filled them to the brim.

Then he told them, "Now draw some out and take it to the master of the banquet."

They did so, and the master of the banquet tasted the water that had been turned into wine. He did not realize where it had come from, though the servants who had drawn the water knew. Then he called the bridegroom aside and said, "Everyone brings out the choice wine first and then the cheaper wine after the guests have had too much to drink; but you have saved the best till now."

This, the first of his miraculous signs, Jesus performed at Cana in Galilee. He thus revealed his glory, and his disciples put their faith in him.

Put yourself in the wedding couple's shoes. It's your big day. You've invited all your closest friends—not to mention that Jesus and His disciples are there also—and the party is in full swing. And now you've run out of wine (which at a Jewish wedding in those days would be a huge embarrassment).

Let's face it. This was a social disaster for this couple. In a matter of minutes, their perfect day was on the verge of being ruined. And they had no way to make their *it* right.

Can you identify with this couple? Can you understand the magnitude of their problem? Have you ever been in a similar situation? You get your paycheck, and before you can spend it, it's gone. You look up and realize there are still thirty days left before you get paid again. One question screams at you: *How am I going to make it?*

I'm sure the bride and groom in this story were asking themselves the same question. *How are we going to make it through the reception with no wine?*

There's nothing worse than having a great need and having no way to meet it. In my travels, I have discovered that there are three kinds of people: those who are going into a situation, those who are coming out of a situation, and those who are in a situation.

Have you thought about where you are currently?

This couple at the wedding was in a situation and trying to find a way out. Thank God, for their sake, because the Way was at the wedding. In John 14:6, Jesus says to his disciple Thomas, "I am the way and the truth and the life." Now what can be more comforting than that, particularly when you absolutely don't know the way on your own?

In the story, Jesus' mother, Mary, appeals to Him to do something that He would continue to do from this moment on—take a broken-down situation, totally hopeless circumstances, completely shattered conditions, and breathe life into them.

I can imagine Jesus being caught off guard. After all, He wasn't there to perform a miracle. He was a guest, or so He thought. He was simply there to enjoy the nuptials with His friends. Then all of a sudden, His mother asks the question of all questions, "Jesus, can You take this bleak and virtually impossible situation and make something marvelous happen?"

Actually, Mary doesn't ask a question at all; she simply makes an observation, "They have no more wine." But Jesus knows what she is saying.

Interestingly, in the text, Jesus tells Mary that His time for miracles hasn't yet come. But as all parents who push their children toward greatness would do, Mary doesn't give up. She doesn't back down. I can just see her standing there with her hands on her hips, giving Jesus a sad, pitiful look that says, *Help now, please.*

When you have a passion for something to happen and you see no way for it to happen without the Son of God Himself stepping in, go to Him with boldness, believing He can make a way for you out of your *no way.* This is what Mary did at the wedding. She not only asked Jesus for help, she also brought the servants to Him and told them to do whatever Jesus said. In addition to having faith that Jesus could solve the problem, she also wanted to make sure He had total cooperation.

How many times have you prayed to Jesus for help, and then resisted when you felt the Holy Spirit leading you toward an answer you didn't want to hear? I know I've done that many times.

Here's a simple truth: If we don't follow God's instructions, we're hindering the great outcome He wants for our lives.

Perhaps sensing that His mother wasn't going to let this go, Jesus finally said, "Fill the jars with water. . . . Now draw some out and take it to the master of the banquet" (John 1:7–8). After tasting what had been drawn from the jars, the master of the banquet realized he was drinking some choice wine. Wow, just like that, nothing turns into something in the Master's hand. A need met, a wedding restored, a miracle performed. Why, you might ask? So we would begin to get the message that nothing is too difficult for God.

Personal Point

My *it* was that I wanted to play in the National Football League. Ask anyone and they'll tell you that the way to get there is by having a dynamic college career. For most guys who aspire to play in the NFL, their senior year in college is the pinnacle of their hopes. At the start of my junior year, I thought I was on the verge. I thought that everything I had worked so hard to achieve was about to happen. And then the bottom fell out—or so it seemed.

Let me take you back to my place of nothingness.

In the fall of 1990, I was the starting running back for the Troy State University Trojans. At the beginning of the football season, I was so thankful that God had allowed me to finally have an opportunity to compete in Division II football. I had taken pit stops at a couple of other schools to put myself in a position to get into a good program such as at Troy. But all the hard times were now behind me, or so I thought. The fans at Troy had nicknamed me "The Mule." They were ready to watch me run the ball.

All I could think about was having two dynamic seasons to establish my name in the minds of the scouts and get on course to be drafted by a pro team.

My junior season arrived, and the hay was in the barn. There was nothing left to do but play. On a warm September night in Orlando, Florida, the Troy State Trojans were preparing for battle against the Black Knights of Central Florida University. My anticipation of the game was unlike anything I'd ever experienced. My heart was racing and my stomach was nervous.

As I suited up, the adrenaline made me ponder many questions. What will we accomplish as a team? Can we get to the postseason? Or will we find ourselves fighting for our football lives each week? How many yards will I gain? How many touchdowns will I score?

I decided that I just needed to remember to concentrate on doing my best on every play.

Thirty minutes before we took the field, my head coach shared with me the most mind-staggering news I could imagine. He told me that at the end of my junior year I would have no more college eligibility at Troy State. In other words, if I stayed at Troy, my junior year would actually be my last year to show the scouts what I could do. I felt like the rug had been pulled from underneath me, and I struggled to find my balance. I had no time to digest it all, however; it was time to play football. But it certainly had my attention.

Later, Coach Maddox explained in detail what had happened. It turned out I had accumulated too many semester hours of credit because of my unconventional road through two other schools to get to Troy State. It wasn't a problem at first, but Troy State had decided to move their program from Division II status to Division I-AA status, which meant that some different rules now came into play. According to these new rules, I had accumulated too many hours of credit to remain eligible.

Suddenly, it looked as if I no longer had a way to reach my dream of playing in the NFL.

Your dream may not be the same as mine, but you may have been in a similar situation. Have you ever been at a point where you think you've finally got it all figured out, and then all at once nothing makes sense? It seems logical to get discouraged at times like these, but you can't let yourself get down. You can't stop pursuing your dream. You have to keep going. You must continue on your path, even when your heart has been broken.

For me, even though I thought I had nothing left, God revealed to me through prayer that I still had the same drive and desire I'd had all along. He'd already taken me to three schools in my quest to make my *it* happen. If He wanted to,

God could still make my nontraditional path successful. I just needed to trust Him and obey Him.

But I didn't understand this right away.

I had a good season my junior year, but off the field I was down pretty low, in a pit of gloom. When the season was over, I realized that returning to school in January, after the holidays, didn't favor my circumstances according to NCAA eligibility rules. Therefore, I decided to sit out in order to preserve one semester of football eligibility. But now what was I going to do? There I was, sitting at home, with no clue of how I could get from where I was to where I wanted to be. I felt like Moses standing at the shores of the Red Sea, trapped, with the water in front of me and Pharaoh's chariots closing in from behind. How could I possibly get across?

Then God reminded me of what Moses said to the people. "Do not be afraid. Stand firm and you will see the deliverance the LORD will bring you today. . . . The LORD will fight for you; you need only to be still" (Exod. 14:13–14).

With seemingly nowhere to turn, I trusted God, and He gave me favor with a family from central Arkansas.

I had met Steve and Carol Shadrach at a Christian conference in Gatlinburg, Tennessee, where they were part of a teaching seminar for a campus ministry they had founded called Student Mobilization. After attending their workshop, I was in awe. When the session was over, I introduced myself to the Shadrachs, and instantly something special began to happen. We just seemed to hit it off.

I kept in touch with the Shadrachs after the seminar, so they were aware of my eligibility situation and were praying for me.

Meanwhile, my coaches at Troy State were trying to help me find a school where I could transfer and still have eligibility to play. One possibility that came up was the University of Central Arkansas. When I mentioned this to Steve Shadrach, he was blown away. It turned out that UCA's campus was only ten minutes from the Shadrachs' house.

Some people would call this a coincidence, but I call it God's divine plan.

Because I still had to sit out the spring semester so as not to use up my eligibility, Steve and Carol asked me if I'd like to move to Arkansas and live with them until the ruling on my situation became official. Through much prayer and my mom's advice, I accepted their invitation.

They took me into their home, and I lived there for the better part of the winter and spring semester. But then another hiccup came. UCA's conference had a residency rule that prevented me from enrolling. So there I was, a Georgia boy living in Arkansas, not knowing what the future held.

Once again I fell back to square one.

Have you ever moved and then found you had to start all over again? You may have wondered, *Why keep trying?* I can tell you from my own experience that God does nothing by accident.

Looking back, I can now see why God led me to live with the Shadrachs in Arkansas. Coming from a single-parent background, I was able to witness what it was like to live in a godly, two-parent home. Although I was raised by an incredible mom, I still had no idea what it was like to have both parents in the home. In Arkansas, I was surrounded by people of tremendous faith. They helped me learn that God works all things together for the good of those who love him (see Rom. 8:28). Though things didn't quite work out for me to play at Central Arkansas, an opportunity soon surfaced in Oklahoma.

Northeastern State University would prove to be the final stop in my college football career. Out of seemingly nothing, God provided me with a great opportunity that I couldn't possibly have imagined. In a span of twelve months, I went from not knowing where I was headed to becoming an All-American football player who would break many records in one sensational senior season.

Are you at a Red Sea in your life? If so, take a page from Moses' life and mine. Understand that bodies of water (no matter how deep and wide) and heart-hardened Pharaohs are no match for God. Are you on a seemingly endless path through the wilderness? Remember, unconventional travels can still lead to the same desired destination. Just place your dreams—your *it*—in God's hands. You may see no results at first, but know by faith that He is doing something dynamic with your *it* and with you.

Inspirational Point

No matter how desolate your situation or how unattainable your goal may seem, never underestimate the power, presence, and position of God. His power is greater than our state of affairs, His presence is in all of our situations, and His position is above all our circumstances. We just have to get Him involved by going to Him as our only resource for survival and our only means for victory.

It's exciting to know that the key to your dreams—both the potential and the likelihood of accomplishing your *it*—lies in the hands of the Master, the Creator of the universe. I hope by now you have come to understand this concept. Before I close this chapter, I want to leave you with three inspirational points that unlock the possibility of the impossible.

■ **1. Believe in your dream.** You may be the only one who does, but you have to believe. As ridiculous as your idea may seem to others, your dream has to make perfect sense to you.

Other people in your life may not be able to grasp your vision. But even when you stand alone, don't be diverted or discouraged. Don't change your mind. And don't ever give up. Understand that the dream itself proves that you already have far more than nothing. That *something* inside you is longing to come out. It's worth fighting for, waiting for, persevering for. When you finally get it in your mind that you've got something worth fighting for, you're one step closer to turning your ambitious dream into reality.

■ **2. Take your dream to God.** Why is God so often a secondary consideration for seeing and obtaining our hopes and dreams? It's almost astonishing to think that we can do it on our own, especially when we consider that God is all knowing, all powerful, and ever present. You would think that those lofty credentials would qualify Him in our minds as a primary resource, but sadly, we all too often look to other people, other places, and other things to do what only God can do.

So take your dream to God, stand on His Word, and know that nothing is impossible for Him. After you release your *it* to God, relax and know He'll make a way out of no way, if it is to be. And if it isn't to be, don't worry. God is doing something in those times too. Either way, you're far from nothing.

■ **3. Obey God's direction.** This can be the most difficult of the three points to actually implement. Sometimes it's hard to follow God. Believe me, I know. Many times He asks us to do some heavy stuff. Sometimes he leads us to do things we're not even sure we can. It's all part of taking up our cross and following Him. Abandoning the familiar isn't easy, even when God calls us to do it.

On the other hand, I've learned the hard way that if we're not willing to do what God says, then we're simply not going to get His assistance. The fact of the matter is that His help is completely available. When God orders our steps and we follow, sweet peace and confirmation comes. He will never lead us astray.

There are mountains that need climbing that only God can help you climb. There are rivers that need crossing that only He can help you cross. And there are impossible circumstances, situations, and problems in life that only He can help you deal with. The key to it all is obedience. Obedience unlocks the door to God's sovereign support.

When you believe in your *it*, bring it to God for His assistance. Obey His plan for your life to help you attain the very thing you're longing for. If you do that, you've mastered the first step in realizing what it takes to achieve greatness.

Smile, God has given you something to hold on to.

Chapter 2

A Little Can Become a Lot
GOD'S MULTIPLICATION PRINCIPLE

Motivational Point

Are you among the many who have something, but in your mind it's not enough? Just enough to lift you, but not enough to carry you. Just enough to feed you, but not enough to fill you. Just enough to save you, but not enough to sanctify you.

If you're among the many who have some but not enough, get ready for some amazing news.

If God can do something with nothing, just imagine what He can do with something.

I hope by now you realize that no matter how bad your circumstances seem, you have *something*. It might be just enough to give you a reason to believe, but not enough to really solve your problem. Just enough to entice you to press on, but not enough to completely fulfill your dream. If you've been waiting and working long and hard to get from nothing to something, I want to caution you to be very careful at this point. It's easy to feel like a fighter in the tenth round of a heavyweight fight, whose corner, out of concern for the fighter's safety, wants to throw in the towel.

Don't do it.

Don't quit now.

You see, you've reached a critical point in the fight where it seems difficult to convert the little bit you have into something more. Maybe you're feeling as if you've knocked on every door, but only sold a handful of magazines, and you still have a whole stack that you need to unload. Or maybe you feel as if you've taken some bitter medicine, but all it can do is treat the symptoms. It never seems to get to the place where it could do some good. If you're like most people, you don't just want a temporary fix; you want the cure. You want the pain to go away and never return.

It's not enough! you scream at the top of your lungs.

And then God whispers back, *It is enough, my friend. It is.*

Having something but not everything can sometimes feel as if you have one can of food and twenty cupboards. But with God, there are always more cans than cupboards. If one can is all you have right now, don't fret, don't waver, and don't give up. Your little bit of something is enough to turn your night into day. It's enough to turn your gloom and doom into joy and celebration.

I could point to many instances in my own life when the little bit I had was more than enough to meet my needs for the moment. All it required was for me to recognize that the same God who could take nothing and turn it into something could surely take something and turn it into more—more than I could ever need and more than I could ever want.

King David, in one of his psalms, says it well:

The LORD is my shepherd, I shall not be in want.
He makes me lie down in green pastures,
he leads me beside quiet waters,
he restores my soul. . . .
You anoint my head with oil;
my cup overflows.

(Ps. 23:1–3, 5)

It doesn't take much for God to turn something into more. As a matter of fact, it takes nothing, and yet here you are with something.

Spiritual Point: Jesus Feeds the Five Thousand (Matt. 14:13–21)

When Jesus heard what had happened, he withdrew by boat privately to a solitary place. Hearing of this, the crowds followed him on foot from the towns. When Jesus landed and saw a large crowd, he had compassion on them and healed their sick.

As evening approached, the disciples came to him and said, "This is a remote place, and it's already getting late. Send the crowds away, so they can go to the villages and buy themselves some food."

Jesus replied, "They do not need to go away. You give them something to eat."

"We have here only five loaves of bread and two fish," they answered.

"Bring them here to me," he said. And he directed the people to sit down on the grass. Taking the five loaves and the two fish and looking up to heaven, he gave thanks and broke the loaves. Then he gave them to the disciples, and the disciples gave them to the people. They all ate and were satisfied, and the disciples picked

up twelve basketfuls of broken pieces that were left over.
The number of those who ate was about five thousand
men, besides women and children.

The numbers just don't add up. Five loaves, two fish,
five thousand people. More demand than supply. By all ac-
counts, this is an unsolvable problem that not even Sir Isaac
Newton could answer.

With most mathematical problems, there's at least a formula for solving the equation. However, there is no formula
to solve this dilemma. The disciples are out of theories,
ideas, and solutions. They simply have more mouths to
feed than they have food.

Which leads to the next obvious question: Where's the
food supposed to come from?

How can you negotiate an extremely high demand when
you have very little supply? If you're a parent, how are you
going to solve the problem of having five mouths to feed
and only one paycheck when the paycheck you have isn't
enough? If you're a businessman, how do you meet your
overhead expenses and pay all your employees when you
can't seem to generate enough revenue to keep the business
open?

Rule number one: don't panic. Don't revert to desperate
measures. Instead, turn your attention to the One who has
the mathematical equation to solve the problem, the One
who has the formula for the dilemma. No, I'm not referring
to your accountant. I'm referring to God, the One who can
make up for your lack.

When they tallied up the available food and came up
with five loaves and two fish, the disciples certainly had
a dilemma. The setting of the sun was drawing near. The
crowds were growing hungry. And yet Jesus was giving

the disciples the responsibility for feeding five thousand people. The disciples wanted to send the people away and make them pay for their own meals. Jesus wanted to meet their need, right there and then. "They do not need to go away," He said. "You give them something to eat."

I can just hear the disciples talking among themselves: What is He talking about? Has He lost His mind? Doesn't He know that it's impossible to feed five thousand people with only two fish and five loaves of bread? It's obvious that He's a carpenter and not a mathematician!

Facing what appeared to the disciples to be an impossible situation, Jesus made the impossible possible. Taking the five loaves and two fish, He looked to heaven and began praying. After praying, He simply began feeding the multitude. As the crowd kept coming, amazingly so did the food. Before long, every belly was filled, and all five thousand men (plus women and children!) had eaten to their satisfaction. Not only did Jesus take the little something they had and multiply it to accommodate the masses, but He also outdid Himself. He also provided enough for the disciples to eat the next day and the day after that.

Perhaps this story has shone a new light on your *it*. I hope it has, because it should. To the disciples, their *it*—the dilemma of not having enough food—seemed like less than enough to do the job, and surely you can see why. Listen to their explanation: "We have only two fish and five loaves of bread." How many times has the word *only* rolled from your lips? If only I had enough money. If only I had more time. Only. Only. Only. Well, the next time you're tempted to say only, remember this: it takes only a little touch from the great multiplier of life to give the increase.

Personal Point

Northeastern State University is located forty miles east of Tulsa, Oklahoma. Certainly you've heard of it. Home of the Mighty Redmen? Okay, maybe you haven't heard of it, but its communications program has earned a measure of fame with its state-of-the-art technology. It's certainly not famous, however, for producing Most Valuable Players of college all-star football games such as the Hula Bowl and the Blue-Gray Classic.

Compared to the Division I football programs at the University of Oklahoma and Oklahoma State, Northeastern was a little fish in a big pond. Make that a little fish in the ocean. We were a small school with a National Athletic Intercollegiate Association (NAIA) affiliation, which meant we were as close to the bottom as we could be.

How was God going to take a little-known football player from a little-known school and produce a two-time Most Valuable Player? How could it possibly happen here at NSU?

Well, if you have God, the bottom is a good place to start.

As far as I know, there hadn't been any previous all-star representatives from Northeastern. So what made me think that I could be the first? Winning the MVP award certainly wasn't on my radar. It would take a monster performance all season to even be considered worthy for all-star selection, let alone outshine all the other stars to be chosen as MVP.

But God had a plan.

During the third game of the season, He created an opportunity for me to break off an eighty-yard touchdown run on an option play against Arkansas Monticello, and after that it was off to the races. By the time we completed our final game, I had rushed for 1,600 yards and fifteen touch-downs. That was enough to attract some national attention. Not only was I named to the All-America team, but I also earned an invitation to the Blue-Gray Classic, at that time held annually in Montgomery, Alabama.

Keep in mind that this was the same player who thought his college career might be over just a few months earlier, when he was sitting stranded in central Arkansas, looking for a place to play.

As you can imagine, winning the MVP award in the Blue-Gray Classic was a major milestone, but an even bigger milestone that year was meeting a beautiful young woman named Stephanie, who later became my wife. Things were looking up!

In the Bible, a young man named David faced a difficult and daunting situation. (Though, in his case, it was liter-ally life or death!) A virtually unknown little shepherd boy, the youngest of eight sons, with no credentials beyond that of keeping his father's flock, David faced one of the great-est challenges ever, going head to head against Goliath, the great warrior from Gath. Goliath stood nearly ten feet tall and had the credentials of a champion.

David, however, was no stranger to competition. On a couple of occasions, he had even faced down a lion and a bear. When David offered to King Saul to go out to face the giant, he said, "Your servant has been keeping his fa-ther's sheep. When a lion or a bear came and carried off a sheep from the flock, I went after it, struck it and rescued the sheep from its mouth" (1 Sam. 17:34–35). Not bad for a shepherd boy!

I had overcome the competition playing at the NAIA level, but I had not faced competition as fierce as I found at the all-star games. These were some of college football's best athletes. Like David, however, who remembered his history with the living God and could say to Saul that the God who had rescued him from the claw of the lion and the bear would rescue him from the hand of the Philistine, I had seen how God had allowed me to succeed against NAIA competition, and therefore I knew He would help me succeed against NCAA competition as well.

And like David, who would go on to conquer Goliath, I conquered the Blue-Gray Classic and Hula Bowl, winning MVP honors in both.

God does not cease to be God in our lives just because the challenges we face are great. If He has done it before—and He has—then He can do it again. There is absolutely no doubt in my mind that God can take your small opportunity and turn it into more opportunity. I know, and so does David. Now what about you?

Inspirational Point

Just when you think your resources aren't enough, God comes along at your request and proves that it doesn't require much from you. When you consider that salvation requires only your belief, but it required Christ's death, you then can truly understand how little your contribution really is. But there are some things you can do.

■ **1. Pray fervently.** Remember that Jesus sought God in prayer before most miracles were ever accomplished. Prayer was a discipline that Jesus practiced continuously. If there is one single way to the heart of God, it is through prayer.

How often do we find ourselves abandoning the most useful and reliable tool in our spiritual arsenal? If your *it* is going to happen, then prayer is the key to unlocking the treasure box.

■ **2. Know your history with God.** Has God ever done anything that you can look back to and say, *Here is where he rescued me*, or, *Here is where He opened the door*? If you're like me, then there is no doubt that you have a history with God that can foster your faith for what you need from God today and tomorrow. Don't forget your history. It's a reliable reminder of God's strength and faithfulness, both for the present and the future.

■ **3. Trust in the Lord.** You serve a God who can be trusted. Proverbs 3:5–6 says:

> Trust in the Lord with all your heart
> and lean not on your own understanding;
> in all your ways acknowledge him,
> and he will make your paths straight.

You might not know how your *it* is going to develop, but trust that God knows. He knows how much, He knows how long, and He knows how many. You can trust God no matter what.

I hope you realize that it doesn't take much with God. The Bible says that faith the size of a mustard seed can move mountains. Do you have mountains that need to be moved? If so, bring your little *it* to God. He can't wait to turn it into something more.

Chapter 3

Make the Right Choice
YOU HAVE TO MAKE A DECISION

Motivational Point

Choices, choices, choices. So many choices and not a lot of room for error. The choices we make shape our lives and affect our futures. It can be as simple as deciding what to wear or what to eat. Or it can be as complicated as deciding where to live or whom to trust. We make choices about the food we eat, which can affect our health. We make choices about the places we go, which can determine how people perceive us. We make choices about our friends and the relationships we enter into, which can affect our character.

The point is that our choices lead us in certain directions, as well as into contact with certain people. What method do we use in making these choices? Or is there no method at all? Maybe you rely on gut feelings or instincts.

I'd like to suggest that our decisions should be well thought out, and most certainly taken to God in prayer. How often have we stayed up hoping and praying that our children will choose the right friends, or that the right friends will choose them? We are never separated from the choices we make.

No matter the situation, our choices do matter. We're not able to remain neutral about anything. Our culture requires that we vote if we want a voice in electing our local and national leaders. As reluctant as we may be about that, we must vote if we want a say in what laws are passed. Not voting also is a choice that has an outcome. Every choice renders a reaction.

I remember my mom getting in my ear before I went to school each day, repeating herself, "Derrick, make good choices today." I suspect that the reason she emphasized good choices was because she expected good results. Therefore, the opposite must also be true: bad choices render bad results. But how often in the course of a day do you remember to think about the consequences your choices will render?

We are all the sum total of the choices we've made and the choices others have made for us. Either way, however, we have the ability to choose where we will go from here. Which way will we choose? Will we choose to trust God, or will we try to pursue our dreams on our own?

Spiritual Point: The Choices of Adam and Eve (Gen. 2:8–9, 15–17; 3:1–7)

Now the LORD God had planted a garden in the east, in Eden; and there he put the man he had formed. And the LORD God made all kinds of trees grow out of the ground—trees that were pleasing to the eye and good for food. In the middle of the garden were the tree of life and the tree of the knowledge of good and evil. . . .

The LORD God took the man and put him in the Garden of Eden to work it and take care of it. And the

LORD God commanded the man, "You are free to eat from any tree in the garden; but you must not eat from the tree of the knowledge of good and evil, for when you eat of it you will surely die.". . .

Now the serpent was more crafty than any of the wild animals the LORD God had made. He said to the woman, "Did God really say, 'You must not eat from any tree in the garden'?"

The woman said to the serpent, "We may eat fruit from the trees in the garden, but God did say, 'You must not eat fruit from the tree that is in the middle of the garden, and you must not touch it, or you will die.'"

"You will not surely die," the serpent said to the woman. "For God knows that when you eat of it your eyes will be opened, and you will be like God, knowing good and evil."

When the woman saw that the fruit of the tree was good for food and pleasing to the eye, and also desirable for gaining wisdom, she took some and ate it. She also gave some to her husband, who was with her, and he ate it. Then the eyes of both of them were opened, and they realized they were naked; so they sewed fig leaves together and made coverings for themselves.

The Bible tells us that the ultimate choice of a lifetime took place in the garden of Eden. A choice so enormous it would affect every generation after it. The ripple effect can still be felt in every city, state, and country, and on every continent. No one is exempt; everyone is included. There are no exceptions based on gender. No exceptions based on race. Everyone is involved. Everyone is guilty.

First, God in His great love created us in His own image. The Bible says, "So God created man in his own image, in the image of God he created him; male and female he created them" (Gen. 1:27). I guess God could have chosen to create us in some other image, but He didn't. He used Himself as a template for what we were going to be. Isn't it amazing that God endowed the human race with the rights and privileges of dominion and superiority (even though, in some cases, we take this a little too far)?

If you read the story of Adam and Eve before the fall carefully, you will discover that they had life as perfect as it could be. God really set them up. He truly blessed them, and said, "Be fruitful and increase in number; fill the earth and subdue it. Rule over the fish of the sea and the birds of the air and over every living creature that moves on the ground" (Gen. 1:28). God also said, "I give you every seed-bearing plant on the face of the whole earth and every tree that has fruit with seed in it. They will be yours for food" (Gen. 1:29). And it was so. The fact of the matter is that God wants us to be His sons and daughters. He wants us as His own. He wants us to remain in fellowship with Him. I emphasize that this is what God wants, but according to Genesis 2 and 3, this is not what God has gotten. No, He's gotten quite the opposite.

Even though God called us to be His, He still gave us a free will to choose Him back. (Now, this is where it gets bad.) There they are, Adam and Eve placed in the garden. They are about to face the greatest dilemma there is, the choice between God and Satan. Adam was given specific instructions about the garden, what to do and what not to do. Also, he knew there would be dire consequences if they did not obey God. "You are free to eat from any tree in the garden; but you must not eat from the tree of the knowledge of good and evil, for when you eat of it you will surely die" (Gen. 2:16–17). What God was telling them was that they could eat what He had provided for them, or they could elect to do their own thing and eat from the tree that He said was forbidden.

Now to add a little twist to the story, it seems they were only influenced toward sin as a result of Satan's presence. I'm going to venture out a bit and suggest that they might not have disobeyed God if Satan hadn't been there. But that's just the problem, Satan was there. He's always there to distract us from God. Why? So he can kill, steal, and destroy. It's really the only way he can do anything to us. He has to get us away from God. And with Adam and Eve, he succeeded. Adam and Eve had a choice—the same choice you and I face every day. Either obey God and remain in His will, or be drawn aside by Satan and watch the ripple effect of sin and evil. Which is it going to be?

Adam and Eve chose Satan. God had chosen them, but they didn't choose God. Why? Before you point your finger at Adam and Eve, take a look at your own daily choices. God or Satan? Who do you choose?

Personal Point

Dealing with an agent was something I had not done before. How do you go about finding one? From what I'd been told, if you were a promising athlete with potential who was on his way to the professional ranks, the agents would find you. Agents made their reputations by the players they represented, by how much money they got for this player or that, or by how difficult they were known to be in negotiations with the teams. They combed the landscape looking for top-notch football talent. From California to Maine, no stone was left unturned. If you happened to be a top player, then your phone was ringing off the hook. The agent's role is to negotiate contracts on the player's behalf and to represent your interests as a professional player.

In my opinion, agents don't get you the opportunity. You have either done that or not, based on your own performance. Agents just know how to talk in a language that general managers of sports franchises are trained to hear.

Choosing an agent is not easy, let me tell you. I had a very difficult time. First, do I make my decision based on the agent's experience, client reputation, or recommendation? Then again, should I be looking at some other factor? Does he have enough tenure in the business, and how many clients does he represent currently?

The first agent I considered had only a small number of NFL players that he currently represented. Naturally, I wondered why. His answer was that he had been in business for only three years. I decided I wanted somebody with a little more experience. Experience was something I thought would be important.

The second agent I interviewed looked promising because he had a very respectable reputation throughout the league. I wanted someone who was well known and well thought of by the general managers. In my research, I found out that agent number two was highly regarded, but I still wasn't sure he was right for me. I decided to talk to a third agent, who had come highly recommended from some reliable contacts. We spent some time together over a two-day period, and I came away with a good sense of who he was as a person as well as an agent.

Finally, after praying and thinking, I had to choose. Would it be agent number one, who was a great presenter but lacked the experience I was seeking? Would it be agent number two, who was second to none when it came to reputation? Or would it be agent number three, who not only came highly recommended, but also possessed other important qualities?

I chose agent number three, and you would not believe how great I felt. I needed to bring this step in the process to a close, and finally I had. No looking back now. It was time to move on to the next phase and allow my agent of choice to do his job.

Finally, the information packages would stop coming. No more phone calls from agents who wanted to meet with me. Still, I was tempted to second-guess my decision, particularly in the first two days. The decision isn't binding until a contract has been signed. I would have to say that my mom was very influential in helping me understand that my choice was indeed the right one. This agent had all the things I was looking for, and I had spent a good bit of time getting to know him. I think most of the second-guessing was because I wanted to be sure I was right. And this was a very big decision.

I thanked God for the opportunity to have a choice. But making the right decision is always a challenge. More importantly, if you have chosen Christ, you have made the right choice. How do I know? Because He chose you first.

Inspirational Point

With your future and mine hanging in the balance, Adam and Eve were faced with the choice of a lifetime. Their decision would ultimately change the course of their lives, and ours! From that moment on, the way they saw each other and God would be different. If only they would have understood the magnitude of their choice!

Have you ever felt that way? If only you had been able to see the true impact of your choices, would things be different? I wonder if Adam and Eve had truly known their condition, would they have disobeyed? Maybe, maybe not. Here are three things to remember when faced with an important choice.

■ **1. Consider whom your decision will affect.** Every decision affects somebody. If it only affects you, to what degree? If it affects others, how will your decision change their lives? Often people who are indirectly affected by a bad choice experience the worst consequences, because they had nothing to do with the decision and thus are uninformed and incapable of doing anything about it.

■ **2. Seek godly counsel.** One thing that so many people fail to do when making a decision is to get counsel. Not just any counsel, but godly counsel that involves a higher standard. When you're making an important decision, it makes sense to get advice and input from someone else who has your best interests at heart.

I wonder if it occurred to Adam to consult with God before he took Eve's advice? The Bible doesn't say what Adam was thinking. It simply says that he took Eve's advice and ate. I wonder how much trouble he could have avoided for himself and Eve—and us!—if he would have checked in with God before taking a bite of the fruit. Here's the point: Don't neglect to ask God Almighty for the direction you need.

■ **3. Consider the consequences.** It really comes down to a question of what will happen if you choose one decision over another. As with Adam and Eve, the path of disobedience is a lesson that every generation has learned while enrolled in the school of hard knocks. No matter how often we fail, God never drops us from the course. He just keeps us enrolled until we pass it.

When making a decision, the moment seems to be the only thing that matters. But truly, a well-thought-out decision involves not only the moment of choice, but all the moments after that, as well. How well have you considered the possibilities? How well have you considered the consequences?

Chapter 4

Prepare for the Storm
RUNNING FOR COVER

Motivational Point

Let's face it, no one really likes being in a storm. We prefer blue skies, calm winds, and favorable temperatures, not the ominous look of inclement weather. If there is anything that can send us into a state of terrifying fear, it is when Mother Nature is in a bad mood. We are no match for her. She's the best at what she does. In some cases, she's difficult to predict and impossible to control. Therefore, we respect her enough to take cover when she gets angry.

When Mother Nature lashes out, it can send us reeling for answers to questions that can't be explained. She is no respecter of persons and has no regard for human life. Her destruction is sometimes all-consuming, leaving only a swath of debris as a reminder of her power. In her wake, life as we knew it is but a memory of what used to be. The cleanup can take years, and in some cases the damage is never fully restored.

Adding insult to injury, there is no one to take to court.

There's no one to blame. One minute she's there, and the next minute she's gone. What do you do with an *it* of this magnitude? According to wisdom, there's only one thing you can do: prepare!

The nature of the potential storm determines the degree of preparation. Hurricanes require an effective evacuation plan. Tornadoes require a firm and steady shelter, preferably below ground. Dust storms force us to keep all the windows and doors shut. The better prepared you are, the more likely your chances of survival.

Up to now, we've been talking about nature, but there are storms of a different kind that also affect our lives. An unexpected diagnosis. An unwanted phone call from the authorities. Downsizing at work. A relationship gone bad.

Whatever the magnitude of the *it*, there is a way to be prepared. Better to be prepared for a storm that never comes than to face a bad situation unprepared. The truth of the matter is that you need to be prepared no matter what the nature of the storm.

I hope you brought your raincoat. The clouds are gathering. The lightning is flashing. The thunder is rolling. It's time to allow the God of the universe to lift you above the storm.

Spiritual Point: Noah and the Ark (Gen. 6:9–7:24)

This is the account of Noah.

Noah was a righteous man, blameless among the people of his time, and he walked with God. Noah had three sons: Shem, Ham and Japheth.

Now the earth was corrupt in God's sight and was full of violence. God saw how corrupt the earth had become, for all the people on earth had corrupted their ways. So God said to Noah, "I am going to put an end to all people, for the earth is filled with violence because of them. I am surely going to destroy both them and the earth. So make yourself an ark of cypress wood; make rooms in it and coat it with pitch inside and out. This is how you are to build it: The ark is to be 450 feet long, 75 feet wide and 45 feet high. Make a roof for it and finish the ark to within 18 inches of the top. Put a door in the side of the ark and make lower, middle and upper decks. I am going to bring floodwaters on the earth to destroy all life under the heavens, every creature that has the breath of life in it. Everything on earth will perish. But I will establish my covenant with you, and you will enter the ark—you and your sons and your wife and your sons' wives with you. You are to bring into the ark two of all living creatures, male and female, to keep them alive with you. Two of every kind of bird, of every kind of animal and of every kind of creature that moves along the ground will come to you to be kept alive. You are to take every kind of food that is to be eaten and store it away as food for you and for them."

Noah did everything just as God commanded him.

The LORD then said to Noah, "Go into the ark, you and your whole family, because I have found you righteous in this generation. Take with you seven of every kind of clean animal, a male and its mate, and two of every kind of unclean animal, a male and its mate, and also seven of every kind of bird, male and female, to keep their various kinds alive throughout the earth. Seven days from now I will send rain on the earth for forty days and forty nights, and I will wipe from the face of the earth every living creature I have made."

And Noah did all that the LORD commanded him.

Noah was six hundred years old when the floodwaters came on the earth. And Noah and his sons and his wife and his sons' wives entered the ark to escape the waters of the flood. Pairs of clean and unclean animals, of birds and of all creatures that move along the ground, male and female, came to Noah and entered the ark, as God had commanded Noah. And after the seven days the floodwaters came on the earth.

In the six hundredth year of Noah's life, on the seventeenth day of the second month—on that day all the springs of the great deep burst forth, and the floodgates of the heavens were opened. And rain fell on the earth forty days and forty nights.

On that very day Noah and his sons, Shem, Ham and Japheth, together with his wife and the wives of his three sons, entered the ark. They had with them every wild animal according to its kind, all livestock according to their kinds, every creature that moves along the ground according to its kind and every bird according to its kind, everything with wings. Pairs of all creatures that have the breath of life in them came to Noah and entered the ark. The animals going in were male and female of every living thing, as God had commanded Noah. Then the LORD shut him in.

For forty days the flood kept coming on the earth, and as the waters increased they lifted the ark high above the earth. The waters rose and increased greatly on the earth, and the ark floated on the surface of the water. They rose greatly on the earth, and all the high mountains under the entire heavens were covered. The waters rose and covered the mountains to a depth of more than twenty feet. Every living thing that moved on the earth perished—birds, livestock, wild animals, all the creatures that swarm over the earth, and all mankind. Everything on dry land that had the breath of life in its nostrils died. Every living thing on the face of the earth was wiped out; men and animals and the creatures that move along the ground and the birds of the air were wiped from the earth. Only Noah was left, and those with him in the ark.

The waters flooded the earth for a hundred and fifty days.

This is one of the most fascinating stories in the entire Bible. Think about it, of all the people on the earth at that time, only one had the television turned to the Weather Channel: Old Man Noah.

There is no doubt that Noah was tuned in when the most accurate and dependable meteorologist of all time gave the most startling weather update. God said to Noah, "Seven days from now, I will send rain on the earth for forty days and forty nights" (Gen. 7:4). Now, *that* is a forecast you do not hear every day. Nevertheless, everyone but Noah and his family ignored the warning. They went about business as usual, even in the face of a gathering storm.

Today, there are many people who are tuned in to some other channel. Even when the breaking news interrupts their favorite program, they take no action to prepare for the coming storm or to respond to the warning. Thank God that Noah did. If he hadn't, you and I probably wouldn't be here. Wait, I take that back. We *wouldn't* be here.

You see, it was through Noah and his three sons, Shem, Ham, and Japheth, and their wives that God would reproduce humanity and repopulate the earth after the flood (see Gen. 9:19). What's important to note is that Noah believed the weather report and obeyed God. How many times in life have you had an opportunity to act after being warned and not done so? How often has it been necessary for you to make preparations, and yet you've failed to do so? Then, when it's too late, you discover that if only you had listened and obeyed, the outcome would have been different.

If you are an athlete, maybe there was a time when you were given specific information about an opponent and you failed to do what the coach said. Did your failure to prepare result in a loss? Not only for you, but for the whole team? Maybe you were told in school that an upcoming exam would cover very specific information, information that was critical for your success, and yet you failed to make the necessary preparations that would have helped you to succeed. Did your failure to heed your teacher's advice result in a failing grade?

Noah was different. He not only believed that it would rain for forty days and forty nights, but he also *did* what God told him to do by building the only means of safety that would accommodate his family and all the creatures of the earth. Noah acted immediately. Why? Because when the rains came, it would be too late, and the consequences of disobedience and inaction would be unimaginable.

According to Genesis 6:14–16, God gave Noah some very specific instructions: "Make yourself an ark of cypress wood; make rooms in it and coat it with pitch inside and out. This is how you are to build it: The ark is to be 450 feet long, 75 feet wide and 45 feet high. Make a roof for it and finish the ark to within 18 inches of the top. Put a door in the side of the ark and make lower, middle and upper decks."

And Noah did this. He did everything that God commanded him. How about you? Are you ready for the storm that's about to make its way in your direction? Do you have an evacuation plan? Or do you believe you can ride it out? Either way, hold on tight to the powerful hand of God. Why? Because storms are no match for God. They never have been and they never will be.

Personal Point

No storm could possibly come my way. There was no way I wouldn't be drafted on the first day. I was projected as a potential first-rounder by several so-called draft gurus. Some said the Pittsburgh Steelers would take me. Others said the Philadelphia Eagles. To me it didn't matter. All I wanted was to get that phone call and begin preparing to join my new team and live in my new city. Several people even told me that I would be the first player taken from the state of Oklahoma.

All my training and preparation was done. No more workouts and timed drills and exercises. No more interviews asking me about my character and work ethics. My records and accomplishments spoke for themselves. It was all over and the moment of truth had arrived.

Everyone at Northeastern State was excited. They put together a huge draft celebration in my honor, in anticipation of my being drafted in one of the early rounds on the first day. I think there were more than a thousand people in attendance. And representatives from every media source in Oklahoma were there in full force. It was such a kind gesture on the part of the university, and I was completely surprised. Still, I was ready. My family was watching back in Albany, Georgia, and the moment I had been waiting for since high school had finally arrived. I didn't sleep a wink the night before.

The draft was being projected on three giant televisions.

My agent was standing by the phone, awaiting the call that would determine my future direction. The anticipation escalated when one of the commentators on the draft speculated that the Eagles were about to draft me in the first round. But it didn't happen.

Hours passed and the enthusiasm in the room began to wane. It began to feel awkward as each successive draft pick was announced. As the first day of the draft came to an end, so did the draft party. People began to leave. Cameras began to shut off. And my excitement began to shut down. A storm was brewing overhead, and it was a storm of incredible proportions, an *it* that would register 10.0 on the Beaufort scale of my life.

The second day began with an early rising back at my dorm room. The party that had drawn a thousand people the day before was now down to two, my roommate and me. Seven rounds were completed, and still I was waiting. Finally, the call came. The storm was passing. I had been selected by the Atlanta Falcons.

Have you ever noticed that no matter how bad the storm has been, you get so excited and such a sense of relief when it passes?

Like Noah, I too was prepared for the storm. I had come to know the Lord and had been in a saving relationship through Jesus Christ for about four years at the time of the draft. The time spent growing in my faith and understanding the presence of God in my life made all of the difference on what was otherwise a very difficult day.

The word from God that spoke so deeply to me in the midst of my storm is found in Luke 8:22–25:

> One day Jesus said to his disciples, "Let's go over to the other side of the lake." So they got into a boat and set out.

As they sailed, he fell asleep. A squall came down on the lake, so that the boat was being swamped, and they were in great danger.

The disciples went and woke him, saying, "Master, Master, we're going to drown!"

He got up and rebuked the wind and the raging waters; the storm subsided, and all was calm. "Where is your faith?" he asked his disciples.

In fear and amazement they asked one another, "Who is this? He commands even the winds and the water, and they obey him."

Do you find yourself even now in a storm of some sort with seemingly no way out? Take cover under the umbrella of Christ's protection. He still speaks peace to the storms.

Inspirational Point

Really and truly, the only way to prepare for the storms of life is to look to the One who can calm every storm in your life. Nature was no match for Him on the raging sea. Blindness was no match for Him in the life of Bartimaeus. Disease was no match for Him when He touched the lepers. Scarcity was no match for Him when He fed the five thousand. I could go on and on, and the stories would never end. Here are three inspirational points to help you prepare for life's storms.

■ **1. Do your homework.** There could be a pop quiz in the morning. You never know when a homework assignment will prepare you for a quiz the next day. You never know when the tests in life will come. You never know when you'll need the answers. But you do know this: Jesus is the answer to life's questions. Develop your faith by studying

God's Word. His Word will help you get through the storms, no matter the degree or magnitude.

■ **2. Remember your notes.** The Word of God memorized is a powerful thing. Committing God's Word to memory is a source of comfort and confidence. The more Scripture you can put to memory, the more effective it will make you when those larger-than-life moments come to your doorstep. His Word becomes our shelter when the wind and rain intensify.

■ **3. Wake the Master of the raging sea.** I love the way Luke tells the story in Luke 8:24: "The disciples went and woke him." Isn't it comforting to know that right there in the stern of the boat is the very One who can say, "Peace, be still"? At times when we feel that it's too much to bear, we can take a stroll to the lower cabin and give the Storm Silencer a little shake. Trust me, He will wake up. Not because the storm is so fierce, but because He loves you so much.

Chapter 5

Understand Your Hope
FAITH THAT RAISES THE DEAD

Motivational Point

To me hope means having an overwhelming peace every day. What can possibly give us a reason for hope in the midst of challenging circumstances? What makes us believe our *it* can become a reality? Especially when it seems so hopeless. To judge by what we see in our society, hope is sometimes an elusive concept.

Let's face it, it's often easier to give up, quit, throw in the towel, blow the whistle, or walk away than it is to have hope. But don't do it. Why? Because when you're pursuing your dream, your *it*, you can't afford to be hopeless. But genuine hope, authentic hope, can only be experienced through a relationship with Jesus Christ.

You see, it's the object of our hope that makes the difference, not the subject. Oh yes, it's easy to get caught up in the subject—the job we need, the illness that has gripped our lives, the family member who has gone astray. Whatever the subject of your concern, never mind it. The subject will destroy your will to want to go on. It will drain you of every ounce of possibility and desire. What do you do when the doctor says there's no cure? What do you do when the roster is posted and you didn't make the team? What do you do when the relationship you've invested in falls apart? I'll tell you what you do. You understand your hope.

If you want the kind of hope that can weather any storm, that can climb any mountain, that can endure any situation, there's only one kind of hope to have, the kind that is available through Jesus Christ. As the song says, "My hope is built on nothing less than Jesus' blood and righteousness." If we were truly honest with ourselves and others, we'd have to admit that we sometimes focus all our attention on the thing or situation that we are hoping for, and not necessarily on the person in whom we should be putting our trust—the One who can make what we are hoping for possible.

Hope keeps us going when it seems that our situations or the subjects of our lives are very difficult. To have hope is to be enriched and connected to the source of our need. Hope can't be touched with human hands and can't be seen with human eyes, but we know by faith that it is available and present in every one of our situations. It fosters the kind of peace that is hard for people who don't have hope to understand. But when you have hope in Jesus Christ, there is absolutely nothing that can take it away. That's because the object of our hope supersedes the subject of our hope. Do you understand that?

Spiritual Point: Jesus Raises Lazarus from the Dead (John 11:1–44)

Now a man named Lazarus was sick. He was from Bethany, the village of Mary and her sister Martha. This Mary, whose brother Lazarus now lay sick, was the same one who poured perfume on the Lord and wiped his feet with her hair. So the sisters sent word to Jesus, "Lord, the one you love is sick."

When he heard this, Jesus said, "This sickness will not end in death. No, it is for God's glory so that God's Son may be glorified through it." Jesus loved Martha and her sister and Lazarus. Yet when he heard that Lazarus was sick, he stayed where he was two more days.

Then he said to his disciples, "Let us go back to Judea."

"But Rabbi," they said, "a short while ago the Jews tried to stone you, and yet you are going back there?"

Jesus answered, "Are there not twelve hours of daylight? A man who walks by day will not stumble, for he sees by this world's light. It is when he walks by night that he stumbles, for he has no light."

After he had said this, he went on to tell them, "Our friend Lazarus has fallen asleep; but I am going there to wake him up."

His disciples replied, "Lord, if he sleeps, he will get better." Jesus had been speaking of his death, but his disciples thought he meant natural sleep.

So then he told them plainly, "Lazarus is dead, and for your sake I am glad I was not there, so that you may believe. But let us go to him."

Then Thomas (called Didymus) said to the rest of the disciples, "Let us also go, that we may die with him."

On his arrival, Jesus found that Lazarus had already been in the tomb for four days. Bethany was less than two miles from Jerusalem, and many Jews had come to Martha and Mary to comfort them in the loss of their brother. When Martha heard that Jesus was coming, she went out to meet him, but Mary stayed at home.

"Lord," Martha said to Jesus, "if you had been here, my brother would not have died. But I know that even now God will give you whatever you ask."

Jesus said to her, "Your brother will rise again."

Martha answered, "I know he will rise again in the resurrection at the last day."

Jesus said to her, "I am the resurrection and the life. He who believes in me will live, even though he dies; and whoever lives and believes in me will never die. Do you believe this?"

"Yes, Lord," she told him, "I believe that you are the Christ, the Son of God, who was to come into the world."

And after she had said this, she went back and called her sister Mary aside. "The Teacher is here," she said, "and is asking for you." When Mary heard this, she got up quickly and went to him. Now Jesus had not yet entered the village, but was still at the place where Martha had met him. When the Jews who had been with Mary in the house, comforting her, noticed how quickly she got up and went out, they followed her, supposing she was going to the tomb to mourn there.

When Mary reached the place where Jesus was and saw him, she fell at his feet and said, "Lord, if you had been here, my brother would not have died."

When Jesus saw her weeping, and the Jews who had come along with her also weeping, he was deeply moved in spirit and troubled. "Where have you laid him?" he asked.

"Come and see, Lord," they replied.

Jesus wept.

Then the Jews said, "See how he loved him!"

But some of them said, "Could not he who opened the eyes of the blind man have kept this man from dying?"

Jesus, once more deeply moved, came to the tomb. It was a cave with a stone laid across the entrance. "Take away the stone," he said.

"But, Lord," said Martha, the sister of the dead man, "by this time there is a bad odor, for he has been there four days."

Then Jesus said, "Did I not tell you that if you believed, you would see the glory of God?"

So they took away the stone. Then Jesus looked up and said, "Father, I thank you that you have heard me. I knew that you always hear me, but I said this for the benefit of the people standing here, that they may believe that you sent me."

When he had said this, Jesus called in a loud voice, "Lazarus, come out!" The dead man came out, his hands and feet wrapped with strips of linen, and a cloth around his face.

Jesus said to them, "Take off the grave clothes and let him go."

Talk about no hope! Mary and Martha were at the lowest level of hopelessness. Lazarus, their brother, has died, and Jesus their Savior is absent. At the outset, Mary and Martha misunderstood their hope. Not that they didn't have hope in Jesus. They just failed to understand the timing of their hope. They thought it mattered for Jesus to arrive in time to save Lazarus while he was still alive. Jesus wanted to teach them that the most important factor was the object of their hope, Jesus Himself, and not the timing or circumstances of their hope.

The message for us to remember is that God is never too late to rescue us from harm and danger. When Martha heard that Jesus was coming, she went out to meet him.

"Lord, if you had been here," she said, "my brother would not have died" (John 11:21). Because she didn't truly understand God's omnipotence, Martha placed limitations on Him. But He has no limitations.

When Jesus said, "Your brother will rise again," Martha replied, "I know he will rise again in the resurrection at the last day" (John 11:23–24).

Martha was talking about one kind of hope, hope in the resurrection at the end of time, but Jesus was talking about a completely different hope, namely hope in His ability to bring Lazarus back to life *right now.*

Mary and Martha didn't understand that their hope for Lazarus could reach beyond his being dead for four days. Their situation limited their hope, but God's power rendered their hope limitless. How often do we place limitations on God? How often do we think that something is impossible, or we don't even entertain the possibility that God can do it, and thus we don't ask Him?

Mary and Martha did not understand the power they had access to through the person of Jesus Christ.

The subject of their hope, the death of Lazarus, had clouded their view of the object of their hope, Jesus, and thus caused them great discouragement and hopelessness. They believed that the next time they would see Lazarus would be on resurrection day, but in a miraculous moment, Jesus reached into the very chambers of the grave and called forth Lazarus.

Then Jesus prayed, "Father, I thank you that you have heard me. I knew that you always hear me, but I said this for the benefit of the people standing here, that they may believe that you sent me" (John 11:41–42).

The Bible says that after Jesus prayed, He called to Lazarus with a loud voice, "Lazarus, come out!" Lazarus, who had been dead for four days, was now alive. Do you have this kind of hope? The kind that can't be restrained, limited, or bound? The kind that is capable of speaking directly into the grave of your circumstances, calling them forth into newness of life? Is your hope in the object and not the subject? If so, then your life, too, can be resurrected.

Personal Point

A dream come true. I couldn't believe that I was actually a member of the National Football League. I wasn't drafted until the eighth round, but I'm thankful that at that time there were twelve rounds in the draft. Today, the draft has been cut back to only seven rounds, so more and more players have to try out as free agents in order to pursue their dream.

After I hung up the phone, I could only sit in my room and take it all in. Not only had I been drafted, but also I'd been selected by the team from my home state of Georgia, the Atlanta Falcons. I was in awe because I'd watched them so much as a young boy. I began thinking about how easy it would be for my mom to come up and see me play. My friends from high school could come as well.

It was also amazing how my disappointment at not being selected on the first day quickly turned into excitement. The draft was behind me, and the challenge of making the Falcons' roster was my next order of business.

Make no mistake, I understood that being an eighth-round draft choice greatly reduced my chances of making the team. But I couldn't worry about that. All I needed was to prepare myself as well as I could for the chance of a lifetime.

My arrival for training camp in Suwanee, Georgia, was

truly filled with anticipation. The challenge I faced was to compete against four established running backs and a first-round draft pick.

Those practices were tough. There were days when I didn't know how I was going to make it, much less showcase my skills so I could make the team. Five grueling weeks of training camp were unlike anything I'd gone through before. The NFL was intense.

Finally, when the dust settled and the final roster was posted, I found I had made the team—well, almost. I was placed on the practice squad, a group of seven guys deemed worthy enough to keep, but not quite ready to play. How you chose to look at it, as "not on the team" or as "close enough to still have a shot," would determine your state of mind. I was happy to still have a shot.

One of the realities of playing professional football is that there is a sixteen-week schedule. Teams that make it to the playoffs play even longer. So anything is possible. I believed I would get a chance to play. That being said, I was excited to be able to work with an NFL team until my time came to be on the active roster.

Though I started out with the right attitude, I must admit that as the season progressed, I struggled mentally. I wondered why I had been placed on the practice squad. I truly believed that I was as good as the other running backs on the team and had earned the right to a spot on the active roster. Unfortunately, the coaching staff, who made those decisions, disagreed with me.

During this long period of watching and waiting, I kept my focus on Christ. Like the apostle John, who was exiled to the island of Patmos because of the word of God, I tried to endure patiently (see Rev. 1:9). There on my own island of Patmos, God was speaking to me, comforting me, and encouraging me to keep the faith and stay focused on Him. Then one day, I showed up ready for practice and was told that the injury suffered by the starting tailback in the previous game would put him out of action for our upcoming showdown against opponent division rival. The running backs' coach told me that I would be activated to play in the last game of the season. My moment had finally come, and all I could think about was how God had taken such good care of me during this long waiting period.

Not only did He take care of me, but He taught me so much about Himself and revealed things to me that I never could have understood had I been in any other situation. Sometimes God permits difficult circumstances in our lives in order to teach us something. Had I been placed on the active roster, I would not have grown so incredibly, as I did while on the practice squad.

It was during this time of isolation and frustration that God had a chance to teach me important lessons about putting my hope in Him and not in my circumstances. It was during this time of waiting that He caused me to grow spiritually, and all the while He knew His perfect time of delivery. Do you feel exiled from your dream? Are you isolated with your *it*? If so, understand that God wants to give you the ability to hope in Him and not in your situation.

Inspirational Point

The writer of the book of Proverbs says that understanding is a prize to be sought after:

> If you call out for insight
> and cry aloud for understanding,
> and if you look for it as for silver
> and search for it as for hidden treasure,

> then you will understand the fear of the LORD
> and find the knowledge of God.
>
> (2:3–5)

Who doesn't want understanding? I would venture to say no one.

We all want to understand. No matter what, we all want to be in a place where life's not confusing and difficult to figure out. That being said, here are three things to remember.

■ **1. Don't get caught up in the situation.** How discouraging are those situations that dominate our lives? They control us almost completely, zapping the energy from every ounce of possibility. The circumstances of life will never stop visiting us with their constant demands for attention, but we don't have to give them the attention they demand, only the attention they need.

It's like having a newborn baby who screams for attention every waking moment. The mother gives the baby what it needs at the appropriate times, and at other times she lets the baby cry, so as not to develop bad habits. I know it can be difficult not to get caught up in the drama of screaming circumstances, but for your own sake, please don't. There's another answer.

■ **2. Give all your attention to the solution.** It's been said that we know the problems, it's the solutions we need to seek. Focusing on the problem can easily draw us away from the solution. The key to freedom is being able to concentrate on the solution while coping with the problem. It's not an easy task to accomplish, but it's the only way out of the problem.

Christ is the solution to all of life's problems, big or small.

But first you have to give Him your time and your heart so He can begin the work of growing you in ways you could not possibly imagine.

■ **3. Wait patiently.** Somehow, I suspect you were hoping for a different third step. Who likes to wait? Nobody I know, particularly in today's society. We all have microwave agendas. We want it right now. If the cooking instructions say one hour in the oven or twenty minutes in the microwave, which one would most of us choose?

But consider that the old conventional oven allows for more tasteful results. Waiting is not the result of God's slowness; it's a remedy for our impatience. Why wait? Because God is doing some slow cooking that will provide a zesty flavor for your soul. Now isn't that worth the wait?

I am so glad that hope is available for all who seek it. In a world that is filled with despair, hope is the element of life that keeps us optimistic about the future, no matter what the situation or the nature of our circumstances. Your hope should not rest in anything or anyone other than Christ Himself.

Chapter 6

Walls Come Tumbling Down
LOOK OUT BELOW!

Motivational Point

Some walls are long and continuous, such as the Great Wall of China. Others are massive and fortified, such as the walls of Jericho. Walls are designed to keep some things out and other things in. They can hold back armies and can be used as a weapon against attackers. They can be as intimidating as you can imagine. But know this: they can come down.

Maybe you're at a wall in your life. A wall designed to keep you out or to keep you in. It's too long to go around, too high to go over, too deep to go under, and too strong to go through. So how are you going to get to the other side?

Why do you even want to get to the other side? In most cases, it's because what's on this side of the wall isn't what you want or is too difficult to handle. So you wait for the wall to come down and release you from its bondage or let you through to your freedom.

Take a moment and think about your wall. How high

is it? Can you climb it? Can you go around it? Maybe you can go underneath it. No chance, huh? Well, there's only one other option, as is true with most walls in our lives. It simply must come down, be done away with, gone.

I know what you're thinking. *That's easy for you to say, Derrick. You don't have my wall in your life.* And you would be right. But I have walls of my own, and you don't know how massive they are either. But no matter how great, how massive, how overwhelming our walls may be, we know that they must come down.

First, we have to believe that they can come down. And when we believe that they can, they usually do. Not always in the way we plan, but often in ways we didn't plan. For example, have you ever been at your wit's end about how you were going to deal with a particular crisis, and then the solution seemed to appear out of nowhere? I know that's happened to me, and every time I was astonished with the results.

What I like about the coming down part is that I get the opportunity to see it fall. It should motivate you to know that the wall you are facing is coming down someday, and you will be a witness to the destruction. That's one event you want to be sure to enjoy. And everyone who has watched you endure the experience of being walled off will celebrate your freedom right along with you.

Doesn't it sound good to hear that your walls can come tumbling down? And when they do, take a piece of the wall as a reminder for next time. That's what I've done. My life is filled with memorial stones from walls in the past that have come down. From the time that I could understand what I wanted to become, one wall after another collapsed between me and my goal. The very fact that I'm writing this chapter is evidence that some pretty big walls have fallen to the ground.

Spiritual Point: Joshua and the Wall of Jericho (Josh. 6:1–27)

Now Jericho was tightly shut up because of the Israelites. No one went out and no one came in.

Then the LORD said to Joshua, "See, I have delivered Jericho into your hands, along with its king and its fighting men. March around the city once with all the armed men. Do this for six days. Have seven priests carry trumpets of rams' horns in front of the ark. On the seventh day, march around the city seven times, with the priests blowing the trumpets. When you hear them sound a long blast on the trumpets, have all the people give a loud shout; then the wall of the city will collapse and the people will go up, every man straight in."

So Joshua son of Nun called the priests and said to them, "Take up the ark of the covenant of the Lord and have seven priests carry trumpets in front of it." And he ordered the people, "Advance! March around the city, with the armed guard going ahead of the ark of the LORD."

When Joshua had spoken to the people, the seven priests carrying the seven trumpets before the LORD went forward, blowing their trumpets, and the ark of the LORD's covenant followed them. The armed guard marched ahead of the priests who blew the trumpets, and the rear guard followed the ark. All this time the trumpets were sounding. But Joshua had commanded the people, "Do not give a war cry, do not raise your voices, do not say a word until the day I tell you to shout. Then shout!" So he had the ark of the LORD carried around the city, circling it once. Then the people returned to camp and spent the night there.

Joshua got up early the next morning and the priests

took up the ark of the LORD. The seven priests carrying the seven trumpets went forward, marching before the ark of the LORD and blowing the trumpets. The armed men went ahead of them and the rear guard followed the ark of the LORD, while the trumpets kept sounding. So on the second day they marched around the city once and returned to the camp. They did this for six days.

On the seventh day, they got up at daybreak and marched around the city seven times in the same manner, except that on that day they circled the city seven times. The seventh time around, when the priests sounded the trumpet blast, Joshua commanded the people, "Shout! For the LORD has given you the city! The city and all that is in it are to be devoted to the LORD. Only Rahab the prostitute and all who are with her in her house shall be spared, because she hid the spies we sent. But keep away from the devoted things, so that you will not bring about your own destruction by taking any of them. Otherwise you will make the camp of Israel liable to destruction and bring trouble on it. All the silver and gold and the articles of bronze and iron are sacred to the LORD and must go into his treasury."

When the trumpets sounded, the people shouted, and at the sound of the trumpet, when the people gave a loud shout, the wall collapsed; so every man charged straight in, and they took the city. They devoted the city to the LORD and destroyed with the sword every living thing in it—men and women, young and old, cattle, sheep and donkeys.

Joshua said to the two men who had spied out the land, "Go into the prostitute's house and bring her out and all who belong to her, in accordance with your oath to her." So the young men who had done the spying went in and brought out Rahab, her father and mother and brothers and all who belonged to her. They brought out her entire family and put them in a place outside the camp of Israel.

Then they burned the whole city and everything in it, but they put the silver and gold and the articles of bronze and iron into the treasury of the LORD's house. But Joshua spared Rahab the prostitute, with her family and all who belonged to her, because she hid the men Joshua had sent as spies to Jericho—and she lives among the Israelites to this day.

At that time Joshua pronounced this solemn oath: "Cursed before the LORD is the man who undertakes to rebuild this city, Jericho: At the cost of his firstborn son will he lay its foundations; at the cost of his youngest will he set up its gates."

So the LORD was with Joshua, and his fame spread throughout the land.

A fortified city is a city that is not only protected on the outside by a wall, but is also protected on the inside by an army. In approaching Jericho, Joshua had his work cut out for him. It was one thing to penetrate the wall (which, according to Jericho's reputation, was an impossible task), but then Joshua also had to deal with all the soldiers inside the city. For the purposes of this chapter, let's just start with the task of the wall.

Don't you find it interesting that the people of Jericho must have known that the wall could come down? Because if it couldn't, why did they need an army? When you see an army amassing on the other side of your wall, take heart. It means the wall can come down! Another great sign that your wall is capable of collapsing is that it has collapsed for someone else before. Chances are it can happen again.

Before I go any further, I want you to recognize what Joshua is doing. Do you see it? He is obeying the commands of God, doing exactly what God has instructed him to do. You and I have an instructional manual called the Bible. In it are God's instructions for living. Reading it is a major step in seeing your wall tumble down.

No wonder it was so important for the priests to go ahead of the ark of the covenant. I believe the priests represented a type of Christ—Christ being the great high priest of the church—and the ark of the covenant represented God's moral law.

No wonder those walls had no chance.

You see, when the Lord goes before you, His moral law follows along, providing what you need in order to see the walls come down.

Joshua got up early the first morning. The priests took the ark of the Lord, and seven priests carrying seven trumpets marched in front of the ark of the Lord. While the trumpets were blowing, the armed troops went in front of them, and the rear guard walked behind the ark of Lord. On the second day, they marched around the city once and returned to the camp. They did this for six days (see Josh. 6:12–14).

It's interesting that the day of destruction arrived not on the sixth day, but on the seventh. Seven symbolizes the number of completion. After six days, the Lord said, in effect, *Everything is in place and my commands are carried out to a T. It's time to take Jericho.*

After the priests blew the trumpets a second time, Joshua said to the people, "Shout!" When they heard the blast of the trumpet, the people gave a great shout, and the walls collapsed.

Can you imagine those massive walls collapsing all around that city? One block after another, leaving not one corner standing. Isn't that just how God works? He doesn't just tear down parts of a wall. The whole thing just comes tumbling down.

I know you don't need just some of your wall torn down. You need the whole thing down. Well, don't worry. It can be done. The reason I know is because it's been done before. Just walk in obedience with God and follow His instructions to the letter.

Personal Point

In spite of how hard I had worked, in this case it wasn't paying off. I know what they say, *Hard work always pays off.* But for me, I was the one who was paying. The day I feared more than any other during my time with the Falcons was called cut day. That's the day when one of the coaches, known as The Turk, pays you a visit and reserves you an appointment with the head coach. Oh, and bring your playbook (and that's not so you can go over some plays).

I was in my second year with the team and really believed that what I had accomplished in the preseason was enough to give me a roster spot. I couldn't go back to the practice squad, so I either had to make the team or get released. In spite of a very successful camp, I was released. I didn't understand why.

Maybe they felt they had too many running backs. Or maybe they didn't have enough money invested in me to warrant keeping me. Whatever the reason, the fact remained that I was done as an Atlanta Falcon. A bigger-than-life wall now blocked my view of my dream of a career in the National Football League.

I remember the day clearly, packing my things in a large

used garbage bag, not knowing where I would go from there. The agony of it all was that I had to walk out of the locker room past all the players who had made the team. Nevertheless, I had to somehow collect myself and do it. I remember waving to the guys as I was leaving, and carrying all my personal items in this garbage bag that I had hoisted over my shoulder.

Not only was I waving, but I was smiling as well. To my amazement, God used that moment to win a player to Christ. Two years later, I got a phone call from this particular player in the late hours of the night. He was calling to tell me his testimony about coming to Christ. One of the things he mentioned was the time I was cut by the Falcons and how what he saw in me made a difference in his life.

"No one who had lost his job would be smiling and waving at us," he said. "I didn't know what you had, but I wanted it." Those are some of the most powerful words anyone has ever spoken to me. Even in the midst of my personal challenge, God was still witnessing to people. The wall that I was facing was truly enormous, and I had no way of knowing how to get to the other side, but God was using that wall to build my faith and to call others to faith in Him.

I spent the rest of the night in my apartment, praying and reading God's Word. Early the next morning, my agent contacted me and told me that the Detroit Lions wanted me to come play for them. I could only stand in amazement that God would cause this wall to collapse before my very eyes, leaving nothing but the rubble behind. In only a few hours, I would be seated on a commercial airline en route to Michigan.

I truly believe that God is always working on our behalf. Even when we can't see what He is doing, we can trust that He has a plan for our lives. As you can imagine, when I got the call from the Lions, I rejoiced, and all those who had prayed with me and counseled me rejoiced as well. God causes walls to collapse. Remember that the next time you find yourself facing a wall you can't get past.

Inspirational Point

Some of the more memorable moments of my professional career came when I had to play on the special teams. No one really wants to play on special teams, but for young players in particular, it's often the only way to make the team. The special team that I enjoyed most was kickoff coverage.

Here's how kickoff coverage works: every player except the kicker runs headlong down the field and throws himself into some of the most vicious collisions in all of sports. Our task was to run as fast as we could while attempting to collapse the wall of defenders on the return team and stop the ball carrier. Usually the return team will use its biggest and strongest blockers to build the wall, which is not stationary, by the way; it's always moving. There were three rules for destroying it, and these same rules apply to destroying the walls in your own life.

■ **1. Run as fast as you can.** You have to build up a head of steam if you're going to have any chance of defeating the wall of defenders (or, in your case, the wall in your life). You can't just tiptoe down the field or walk toward this oncoming force. No, my friend, you have to charge it, creating more momentum than the force that is coming at you.

Developing a head of steam is not something that is easily accomplished. Finding the drive and determination to create this momentum can be difficult, especially when you've been shut out for so long. Nevertheless, if the wall's going to come down, you have to hit it with everything you've got, leaving nothing behind. It's going to take every ounce of your concentration and determination. But you can do it. Don't worry about how large it is, just run.

■ **2. Look for a place to penetrate.** Every team has a player or players on their kick return team who represent the weak link in the wall. Through scouting and film evaluation, we had to figure out which guy this was. We looked for things like lack of hustle, undeveloped skills, poor technique, and inconsistent blocking. Ultimately, the players we attempted to expose were our way to destroy the wall.

You have to look for ways to exploit the wall's weakness. They're not easy to find, but they do exist. You just have to evaluate. Keep looking. There are ways to make progress with the walls in your life, ways to figure out how and where to penetrate.

■ **3. You have to finish.** Building up a head of steam and finding the other team's weakness isn't enough if you don't finish by making the tackle. The object of the play is always to make the tackle. Without a tackle, the play isn't successful.

Maybe the "tackle" in your case is to leave no stone unturned, exhausting every option, going the extra mile. The wall may not collapse in the place you thought it would, but it will come down. Maybe you didn't get the job you wanted, but you got the one you needed. Maybe your illness wasn't cured, but it was treated.

When you play on the cover team, you don't always make the tackle. Sometimes, somebody else makes it for you. Likewise, in life, you don't always get what you want. Instead, you get enough to keep you and sustain you in perfect peace.

Chapter 7

Find the Good News

DON'T WORRY, BE HAPPY

Motivational Point

Extra! Extra! Read all about it! It's the lead story in most of today's newspapers. Front page news: "Child abducted from local park." "Amber Alert" messages are posted on the highway, and every motorist who notices the alert begins recording in their minds the description of the car the abductor was driving.

Bad news: "Apartment burns down on Fifth and Broad." An elderly woman is found dead.

Some days, it's one bad headline after another, of the kind of news that no one likes to hear. On the six o'clock news, the lead anchor starts with an opening tragedy—and then follows with four or five more.

But what if the newspaper's lead story each day was about some great achievement, such as the community coming together to revitalize a neighborhood? Or what if the local television news broadcast a story about someone donating an organ to save a person's life? Now wouldn't that be incredible?

It's bad news are three of the most dreadful words we could ever hear. That's an *it* that can completely overwhelm us. In many respects, we live in a world of bad news, and we have to realize that there's a song to sing even then. Right where it hurts the most, there's a place of sweet relief.

How can that be possible? I'll tell you how. It simply comes down to what you know. Knowledge is the key to unlocking the treasure chest of good news. No matter how deep it might be buried or hidden, the good news is in the bad.

Now, before you think I'm crazy, let me explain.

I call it the Blow Pop encounter. Children may understand this example better than adults will, but everyone has had a Blow Pop encounter. You purchase your favorite flavor of Blow Pop. You unwrap it and begin to enjoy that amazing, sweet candy flavor for several minutes, only to discover that the candy is about to be dissolved due to the constant licking. No more candy. No more licking. No more fun. Bad news.

Hidden inside the bad news of the diminishing Blow Pop, however, is the incredible presence of chewy bubble gum. If you remember from your Blow Pop-eating days, the gum seemed even sweeter than the candy. Not to mention the bubbles you could blow.

So, what is the good news hidden inside all the bad news in our world? It's the good news of the gospel of Jesus Christ: He has come to save the world from its sin. And what that means is that we have a future ahead of us that is beyond our wildest dreams, which is what makes it possible for us to sing the good news amid all the chaos.

The apostle Paul says in Ephesians 1:15–19, "Since I heard

about your faith in the Lord Jesus and your love for all the saints, I have not stopped giving thanks for you, remembering you in my prayers. I keep asking that the God of our Lord Jesus Christ, the glorious Father, may give you the Spirit of wisdom and revelation, so that you may know him better. I pray also that the eyes of your heart may be enlightened in order that you may know the hope to which he has called you, the riches of his glorious inheritance in the saints, and his incomparably great power for us who believe. That power is like the working of his mighty strength."

There it is. We found it. The reason we can sing is hidden in the person of Jesus Christ, and this gives us our reason to sing no matter how bad the news is.

Spiritual Point: Paul and Silas Singing in Prison (Acts 16:16–25)

Once when we [Paul, Silas, and their traveling companions, including Luke] were going to the place of prayer, we were met by a slave girl who had a spirit by which she predicted the future. She earned a great deal of money for her owners by fortune-telling. This girl followed Paul and the rest of us, shouting, "These men are servants of the Most High God, who are telling you the way to be saved." She kept this up for many days. Finally Paul became so troubled that he turned around and said to the spirit, "In the name of Jesus Christ I command you to come out of her!" At that moment the spirit left her.

When the owners of the slave girl realized that their hope of making money was gone, they seized Paul and Silas and dragged them into the marketplace to face the authorities. They brought them before the magistrates and said, "These men are Jews, and are throwing our city into an uproar by advocating customs unlawful for us Romans to accept or practice."

The crowd joined in the attack against Paul and Silas, and the magistrates ordered them to be stripped and beaten. After they had been severely flogged, they were thrown into prison, and the jailer was commanded to guard them carefully. Upon receiving such orders, he put them in the inner cell and fastened their feet in the stocks.

About midnight Paul and Silas were praying and singing hymns to God, and the other prisoners were listening to them.

Doesn't it always seem to be the case that when you are minding your own business, trouble has its own funny way of showing up in your life? Seemingly, you have no problem that you can think of and life is just wonderful. Then, in the blink of an eye, that which was so peaceful becomes chaotic. Such was the case with Paul and Silas in the city of Philippi.

It says that Paul and Silas were on their way to prayer. Can it be any more peaceful than that? But then it says that a slave girl met them who had a spirit of prediction and made a large profit for her owners by telling fortunes. Can it get any more chaotic than that? From calm to chaos in a matter of moments, and Paul's and Silas's lives are about to take a huge turn.

As the girl followed Paul and Silas, she cried out, "These men are servants of the Most High God, who are telling you the way to be saved." And she did this for many days, until Paul became greatly aggravated. Finally, he turned to the spirits and said, "In the name of Jesus Christ I command you to come out of her!" And they came right out (see Acts 16:17–18). Well, it didn't take much for the girl's masters to recognize that Paul was interfering with their business plan. Have you ever interrupted the plans of someone who was living to please themselves? If so, you know that it didn't go over too well, and chances are you weren't very popular for interfering.

When the girl's owners saw that their hope for profit was gone, they seized Paul and Silas and dragged them into the marketplace to face the city authorities. Do you remember that bad turn I spoke of earlier? Well, this is *it*. Paul and Silas are now in an unfortunate situation that's getting worse by the second.

In their testimony before the magistrates, the slave owners said, "These men are ruining our city." Isn't it interesting that they accused them of disturbing the whole city, rather than sticking to the facts of the case? Based on those trumped-up charges, Paul and Silas were stripped of their clothes and beaten with rods. Finally, they were thrown into a cell at the inner core of the jail.

If you're going to find a song to sing, it's going to come down to your knowledge of God, not your situation. Paul and Silas were in a bad situation, but they had knowledge of their relationship with God and truly understood His presence and power in their lives. For me, even with everything I know about God, I'm still in awe of what Paul and Silas understood and how it transformed their attitude.

Think about it for a moment. Paul and Silas are not at a barbecue surrounded by friends. They are in a stinky, filthy jail cell—with no way out. Now that I think about it, though, I'm not so sure they were even seeking a way out. I say that, because something about their being in this bad-news situation moved them to sing. This must have been quite a song, because the passage tells us that it was late when Paul and Silas were singing hymns to God, and out of this singing, the most powerful event was taking place: the other prisoners were listening to them. Even in their most difficult moment, Paul and Silas were still witnessing on God's behalf, and people were still being saved.

Can you see how incredible it is to have the knowledge of God? If you take the time to read the rest of the story, you will discover that Paul and Silas were freed from the cell and everybody who was in chains was freed. You will also discover that the jailer was amazed. He fell down trembling before Paul and Silas and said, "Sirs, what must I do to be saved?" The next time you get some bad news, hang in there. The good news is just beneath the surface.

Personal Point

After being released by the Falcons, I was disappointed. But when my agent called me to say I'd been picked up by the Detroit Lions, I was excited about having a new opportunity. But there was one little concern that made me have some reservations about my new home. That concern was named Barry Sanders.

In my own words, Barry Sanders was simply the best running back in the game at the time—and quite possibly, when it is all said and done, he could go down as the best ever. At 5'10" and 200 pounds, he had the most incredible ability to cause defenders to miss tackles. He could cut on a dime in any direction, seemingly without limitations. No space was too small and no angle was to his disadvantage. Just when you thought you had him—guess again. You never had him; he always had you.

I remember a particular game against the Green Bay Packers. The Pontiac Silverdome, our home field, was packed to the rafters—80,000 fans, and as loud as you can imagine—and every fan was holding a sign that said, "Barry! Barry!" The play was called 37 Stretch. We were on our own twenty-five-yard line. Barry took the handoff and ran the stretch play to the left. Immediately, three Packer defenders collapsed on him—one to his right, another to his left, and the third guy in front. Seemingly, there was nowhere to go.

Now, what I'm about to tell you is absolutely mind boggling. Not even Houdini could have escaped from this situation.

There was only one way to go. You guessed it: backward. What we saw next from the sidelines was not physically possible. In an instant, Barry came to a complete stop and backed up, freezing the defenders while creating some space between him and them. Then, with a lightning quick cut, he was able to get to the perimeter, and from there, there was no stopping him. He scored on a seventy-five-yard run. To this day, I still don't believe what I saw. He was simply the best.

So for me, the idea of going to Detroit turned some bad news (being released by the Falcons) into what seemed to be worse news. How was I ever going to get any playing time in Detroit? And starting was completely out of the picture. Anywhere else, maybe there would have been a chance. But in Detroit? No way. Or at least I thought there was no way. To my amazement, however, God once again gave me a reason to sing. In the conversation I had with God as I was making my way to Detroit, I said, "I can't see how I can possibly see any playing time." But God has His ways.

Thanks to Dan Henning, the Lions' offensive coordinator, a way was created. I found out that the coaches had seen what I could do in short-yardage and goal-line situations. Therefore, during those times in the games when we needed one or two yards, they usually took out the best running back in all of football and entrusted to me the task of succeeding in those situations. And succeed I did.

But God wasn't through. In what I believed to be the sovereignty of God, Barry Sanders had not missed a game in five years. During my first season with Detroit, however, he was injured for the first time and had to be replaced for seven weeks. Now, I certainly didn't want to get my opportunity like that. You never want to see anyone injured, not to mention the best player in football. But guess who replaced him? Yours truly. God reminded me of our conversation on the airplane. He said, "You told Me you wouldn't play in Detroit. Seems to Me you're doing more than playing; you're starting."

I simply could not believe it. God turned bad news—and even worse news—into good news. So don't get silent when the bad news shows up. Instead, start warming up your vocal cords like Paul and Silas did. Just start praying and singing hymns to God. The good is on the way.

Inspirational Point

I want you to know and understand that what you just read is not an attempt to ignore the facts of what you're dealing with, or to suggest that bad news is ever easy to face. I'm not asking you to go through some sort of denial of the issue. I simply want you to recognize that there is a peaceful method of coping with bad news. Not only is it a peaceful method, but it's a successful method. As an encouragement and a reminder, let me suggest three things for you to remember.

■ **1. Don't panic.** Why? Because you don't have to. Knowing that you serve a great God, and that He cares greatly for every event in your life, can and will allow you to cope with the situation. I know I'm asking a lot, but thank God you don't have to deal with the bad news alone. Jesus said, "In this world you will have trouble, but take heart! I have overcome the world" (John 16:33). Part of "overcoming the world" means He has also overcome the bad news you are facing.

■ **2. Don't be afraid.** The Bible says, "God has not given us a spirit of fear, but of power and of love and of a sound mind" (2 Tim. 1:17 NKJV). Jesus often told his disciples, "Do not be afraid," or, "Fear not." I conclude that the reason He did this was because He knew they were afraid. So when I say, "Don't be afraid," I'm simply echoing Jesus' words. Your situation did not catch God by surprise. He was not shocked to see things turn out the way they have for you. He is very much familiar with the situation. If you look closely at your situation, you will find that God is directly in the middle of it, and He's saying, "Don't be afraid."

■ **3. Be courageous.** Isn't it interesting that we typically define the word *courage* by describing it in contrast to fear? Courage has a way of surfacing while we are going through difficulties. We don't find courage apart from problems; instead, we find it in the midst of problems. Courageous people often become courageous and demonstrate feats of courage when they are faced with something bad and fearful. Courage, in part, is our ability to overcome fear.

Paul and Silas were right in the middle of a bad and discouraging situation. And I would imagine they felt a bit of fear. But it was in the midst of those same fearful circumstances that they found the courage to sing—and oh, what a song it must have been. Any time your singing can cause an earthquake and shatter the shackles that are keeping you bound, it must be quite a song. So I encourage you to sing. And don't stop until something good happens.

Chapter 8

Fix Your Own House First

IT STARTS WITH YOU

Motivational Point

Sometimes it's not a bad idea to do some renovations. You know what I mean by "renovation," don't you? Around the house, it means changing the tile to carpet, upgrading the laminate countertops to granite, or replacing an old, worn-out roof. Maybe sometimes it means moving a wall or two to make things more open.

When it comes to our circumstances, "renovation" can mean changing our attitude or our perspective to be more open to seeing and accepting God's work in our lives. Whatever you need to do to renovate your life, I suggest you get to it.

I won't ever forget helping my in-laws with some renovations. I don't know if you've ever had to pull up old carpet, but if not, I want you to know it's not easy. If you have, you know what I'm talking about. My in-laws had carpet almost everywhere in their four-bedroom, two-and-half-bath ranch home. The only place they didn't have carpet was in the kitchen. After realizing how much work was ahead for me, I suggested to my brother-in-law that he should encourage his parents to leave the carpet in place and we could just clean it really well, but to no avail. It had to come up.

The first thing we discovered was that the carpet and pad were glazed to the floor, and the only tool we had was a flat, shim-like item used for scraping tile. We had to get underneath the edge of the carpet and push back and forth between the carpet and the floor. As the carpet separated from the floor, we had to lift it and pull it. Good grief, I'm getting tired just writing about it. Finally, when all the adhesive had been separated, the carpet would show no more resistance, and the work would come to completion.

I've come to discover that the renovation process is strikingly similar to what takes place in our lives. We sometimes need renovating. Now, it's very easy to see where someone else could use a little work, but we seldom look at our own lives and see the same things. Let the truth be told—there is a little carpet upheaval that needs to happen in our own lives as well.

It's awfully easy to recognize that someone else has a problem when you could have a problem with the same thing. For example, you might look at someone else and say they're "dishonest," whereas in your own life, you call it "a little white lie," you know, practically harmless. What you fail to realize is that there is no such thing as "a little white lie." But the most important thing is to see that you might be suffering from the same problem you're criticizing in somebody else's life.

Now the obvious question arises. How do you fix your problem first? The answer is very simple—you just have to admit that you have the same problem. Sounds simple, but no one enjoys admitting they have a problem. It's really quite similar to our need to realize that we need a Savior as the first step toward restoring our separation from God. If we never recognize that we have a need, we can never truly enter into the relationship.

Remember, we need to start with ourselves first. Don't worry about your neighbors' houses and all their obvious problems. Start with your own problems first.

Spiritual Point: A Woman Caught in Adultery (John 8:1–11)

Jesus went to the Mount of Olives. At dawn he appeared again in the temple courts, where all the people gathered around him, and he sat down to teach them. The teachers of the law and the Pharisees brought in a woman caught in adultery. They made her stand before the group and said to Jesus, "Teacher, this woman was caught in the act of adultery. In the Law Moses commanded us to stone such women. Now what do you say?" They were using this question as a trap, in order to have a basis for accusing him.

But Jesus bent down and started to write on the ground with his finger. When they kept on questioning him, he straightened up and said to them, "If any one of you is without sin, let him be the first to throw a stone at her." Again he stooped down and wrote on the ground.

At this, those who heard began to go away one at a time, the older ones first, until only Jesus was left, with the woman still standing there. Jesus straightened up and asked her, "Woman, where are they? Has no one condemned you?"

"No one, sir," she said.

"Then neither do I condemn you," Jesus declared. "Go
now and leave your life of sin."

What a peculiar situation Jesus finds himself in here,
surrounded by a crowd that was prepared to be taught by
the Messiah, only to discover that the lesson would be of
extreme magnitude. No, this wasn't basic math or simple
science. This was a school of advanced and higher learning. Also enrolled in the class were attorneys and theolo-
gians of the law. The case: What to do with someone caught
in blatant sin.

After a night on the Mount of Olives, Jesus "appeared
again in the temple courts, where all the people gathered
around him, and he sat down to teach them. The teachers
of the law and the Pharisees brought in a woman caught in
adultery" (John 8:2–3). The obvious questions arise: Where
was the man she was caught with? Why is she the only one
they brought in? By the law, one was as guilty as the other.
Both could be put to death. Could it be that the man was
also a part of a plot to trap Jesus? Jesus must have realized
this, but he didn't question them about the whereabouts of
the man, who should have been brought before him as well.
With all ears open and eyes fixed on Jesus, they ask the life
or death question: "Teacher, this woman was caught in the
act of adultery. In the Law, Moses commanded us to stone
such women. Now what do you say?" (John 8:4–5).

It must have been dead silent when the question was answered. A question of this degree was too difficult to handle,
particularly when you consider the Pharisees' intentions. If
Jesus agreed that she should be stoned, He would be going
against the Roman law, which forbade the Jews from carrying out capital punishment. If He tried to release her, He
could be faulted for ignoring the words of Moses. If ever it

seemed that anyone was caught between a rock and a hard place, it truly was Jesus. Or so they thought. Can you imagine the Rock of all ages being caught between a rock and a hard place? The Bible says that He bent down and started to write on the ground with His finger. Then He straightened up and said, "If any one of you is without sin, let him be the first to throw a stone at her" (John 8:7).

Wait a minute. That's not what we were thinking, the attorneys and Pharisees must have thought. Like a deer caught in the headlights, they were frozen in their tracks and could do only one thing: drop the stones and walk away.

How else do you respond to such a profound statement? Truly all of us have sinned and deserve death, be it by stoning or however. But we no longer stand condemned as a result of our sin. We no longer are condemned to die in our sin according to the punishment of sin. Roman 6:23 says, "For the wages of sin is death, but the gift of God is eternal life in Christ Jesus our Lord."

Funny how the Pharisees, in their scheme to trap Jesus, forgot where they had placed the trap and got caught in it themselves.

Personal Point

What happened with the Lions paved a road from Detroit to San Francisco. This is *it!* The one opportunity I had been seeking from the time I was drafted back in 1992. The opportunity to be a starting running back in the National Football League. No longer a practice squad player waiting in the wings to move up to the active roster. No longer in the shadow of the great Barry Sanders. It was my time and hour to be the man.

You may ask, Why San Francisco? Home of the four-time (now five-time) Super Bowl champions, with players such as Joe Montana, Jerry Rice, Steve Young, and Ricky Watters. Why would the 49ers be interested in a running back who had never been a starter and had never been to the Pro Bowl? I'll tell you why. First, they were going to be losing Ricky Watters to free agency, which meant he was no longer 49er property. Ricky was one of the most versatile players to play the running back position. He could obviously run with great ability, and he also possessed the ability to catch the ball out of the backfield with exceptional skill.

Why is that important? Well, if you were going to play in the West Coast offense developed by 49er coach Bill Walsh, you had to have the ability to do both. In the previous season, during a Monday night game, I had played against the 49ers while Barry Sanders was out with an injury. I had no idea that my performance that night would open up an opportunity for me the following season. I ran with reckless abandon and caught the ball out of the backfield extremely well. The 49ers were so impressed with my performance that, as soon as Ricky Watters became an unrestricted free agent, they made contact with the Detroit Lions to inquire about my becoming a 49er. The 49ers gave the Lions a fourth-round selection in the upcoming draft in exchange for my services. Just the mere fact that I was being wooed by the world champion 49ers was a sign that only God could have made this opportunity possible. The biggest *it* of my career had arrived. And the sovereign hand of the Lord made it possible.

I had often wondered while working on the practice squad with the Falcons and backing up Barry Sanders in Detroit, *What could I do if I were given the starting role?* That being said, the 49ers experience was like no other. The opportunity was great, but the timing was bad. They were coming off a Super Bowl win and they certainly wanted to repeat. Ricky Watters was gone, and the microscope focused on his replacement was going to be magnified.

Unfortunately, I soon found that the West Coast system was going to take me some time to get comfortable in. But time was not what the 49ers had. They felt they needed someone who could balance his attack with running and catching. And what I wanted to do was tip the scales more toward running than catching. They wanted one thing and I offered something else. Consequently, I was released after training camp. The experience certainly taught me a lot about what I didn't know about my position. What I needed to learn was to maximize my opportunity by being able to do both run and catch passes out of the backfield. Nevertheless, my time in San Francisco sure was fun. As brief as it was, what an opportunity it was to have been on the same team with the likes of Steve Young and Jerry Rice.

When I think back on that moment, the thing I treasured the most was the opportunity to share my faith with several players and live out before them the Christian experience. Who knows? Maybe they learned as much from me as I did from them.

Inspirational Point

I'm still amazed to this day that God allowed me to reach the pinnacle of opportunity after starting from a place of very little opportunity. God used these experiences to show me and teach me the principles of always learning and becoming as knowledgeable in my craft as I could. In particular, I learned three points to remember.

■ **1. Don't point at others until you've pointed at yourself first.** Usually, if you start here, you won't have to go any further. As the saying goes, "When you point a finger at someone else, there are three fingers pointing back at you." I don't know who first said that, but they sure did make a good point. We all have enough need for renovation in our own lives, so we don't need to spend time trying to renovate someone else.

The Pharisees had their own sin to contend with, and Jesus just did a terrific job of causing them to consider themselves as sinners. They were no different from the woman they brought charges against. When you get down to it, what Jesus was really saying was that anyone can pick up stones, but nobody can throw them, because we all have sinned.

■ **2. Admit that you too may suffer from the same tendency to sin.** At the beginning of the story, the Pharisees were all indignant as they dragged the woman caught in adultery to face Jesus. By the end of the story, each and every Pharisee had acknowledged that he too was a sinner. That was evident in their dropping of the stones they had initially picked up to stone the woman, and by their walking away, no longer willing to accuse her. No argument, no debate, no question. They knew Jesus was right and they were wrong.

Isn't it also interesting that of all the teachings of Jesus the Pharisees heard, they understood the one about sin more than any other? It kind of makes you wonder why Nicodemus was the only one who really seemed to get the full picture and come to faith in Jesus. The others were always ready to condemn others for breaking the law, but never themselves.

■ **3. Jesus and you are the only ones left to deal with your sins.** When you think about it, our sins can only be rectified by Jesus Himself. No one else can pardon us or excuse us. As a matter of fact, no one else is capable of forgiving us.

Of all the religions of the world, there is but one that provides an answer for what to do with our sins. And believe me, something must be done with our sins. Fortunately, something has been done with them. Jesus carried them with Him to Calvary.

Chapter 9

You *Can* Make a Difference
A LASTING IMPACT

Motivational Point

If there's anything I have learned over the years, it is that you can never underestimate the power of the human spirit. Just when it seems there is nowhere else to go, something in our spirit says, *Go this way.* Just when you want to quit, there is something that says, *No, you can do it.* Whatever that thing is, you know you have it when the moment calls for it. And for those of us who have experienced it, what a blessing.

There are times when you think you are at the end of your rope. What you need is more rope, and amazingly, more rope appears. Who can truly explain why some people have an incredible ability to reach deeper than others? It's been said that, where some of us end, others begin. The others I am referring to are those who refuse to accept that they have nothing else to give or nothing else to contribute. They won't settle for not leaving their signature on the canvas of a situation. Maybe that's what it is—they just have to finish stronger than they began.

These people are called difference makers. They're the kind of people who walk into a room and brighten the whole place up. They walk into a situation and leave it better than what it was before. How can you become a difference maker? You have to get around people who are making a difference. You have to discover it by experience.

The desire to make a difference is a desire that needs fueling. If desire represents a motor vehicle, and that special something that makes a difference is the fuel, then it becomes easy to understand. The car doesn't run without the fuel. Neither does the human spirit.

The fuel I'm speaking of, the fuel that makes the difference, and the fuel that can empower *you* to make a difference, is the Word of God. The difference is His Word. When you get into the Word, it gets into you. When it gets into you, the difference is automatically recognized by others and shows up at the most critical moments.

Some of us have the desire, but we haven't filled up with the fuel. In order to get to certain levels, to do certain things, we need a full tank and constant refueling.

Let me ask you a question. Do you see yourself as a difference maker? An impact performer? Are you the type who can leave a lasting impact on all those you encounter and become the difference maker that charts a whole new course? The key to traveling beyond the mundane is the fuel and not the car.

Spiritual Point: Esther Has the Courage to Save Her People (Esther 4:1–17)

When Mordecai learned of all that had been done, he tore his clothes, put on sackcloth and ashes, and went out into the city, wailing loudly and bitterly. But he went only as far as the king's gate, because no one clothed in sackcloth was allowed to enter it. In every province to which the edict and order of the king came, there was great mourning among the Jews, with fasting, weeping and wailing. Many lay in sackcloth and ashes.

When Esther's maids and eunuchs came and told her about Mordecai, she was in great distress. She sent clothes for him to put on instead of his sackcloth, but he would not accept them. Then Esther summoned Hathach, one of the king's eunuchs assigned to attend her, and ordered him to find out what was troubling Mordecai and why.

So Hathach went out to Mordecai in the open square of the city in front of the king's gate. Mordecai told him everything that had happened to him, including the exact amount of money Haman had promised to pay into the royal treasury for the destruction of the Jews. He also gave him a copy of the text of the edict for their annihilation, which had been published in Susa, to show to Esther and explain it to her, and he told him to urge her to go into the king's presence to beg for mercy and plead with him for her people.

Hathach went back and reported to Esther what Mordecai had said. Then she instructed him to say to Mordecai, "All the king's officials and the people of the royal provinces know that for any man or woman who approaches the king in the inner court without being summoned the king has but one law: that he be put to death. The only exception to this is for the king to extend the gold scepter to him and spare his life. But thirty days have passed since I was called to go to the king."

When Esther's words were reported to Mordecai, he

sent back this answer: "Do not think that because you are in the king's house you alone of all the Jews will escape. For if you remain silent at this time, relief and deliverance for the Jews will arise from another place, but you and your father's family will perish. And who knows but that you have come to royal position for such a time as this?"

Then Esther sent this reply to Mordecai: "Go, gather together all the Jews who are in Susa, and fast for me. Do not eat or drink for three days, night or day. I and my maids will fast as you do. When this is done, I will go to the king, even though it is against the law. And if I perish, I perish."

So Mordecai went away and carried out all of Esther's instructions.

This is truly one of the greatest stories of the Bible. If you have never taken the time to read it, you should. If you have never even heard of it, then it's time to get acquainted with it. The book of Esther is ten chapters of an incredible tale about a woman who courageously acted on behalf of her people, in spite of what she was facing. King Xerxes (or Ahasuerus, depending on which English translation you're using) of Persia ruled over 127 provinces, stretching from India to Ethiopia. In his third year as king, he held a feast for all of his officers and staff. For six months, he displayed his wealth and splendor. Isn't that just what we do when we come into great wealth?

The queen also had a feast with which she entertained the women of the palace. At the end of the week of drinking and dining, the king requested that Queen Vashti be brought before him. But the queen refused to come at the king's command. Now, one thing I've learned over the years is that not doing what those in authority tell you to do will get you into more trouble than anything. Queen Vashti's refusal only fueled the king's anger. After consulting with his high officials, the king decreed that Vashti should never again enter the king's presence and her royal position should be given to another woman who was more worthy than she. The king was concerned that word would get out about Queen Vashti's refusal, and the royal officials didn't want the other women of Persia responding in the same way to their own husbands.

A Jewish man named Mordecai was living in the fortress of Susa, which was also occupied by the king. Mordecai had taken on the responsibility of caring for his niece Hadassah, or Esther. Esther's parents had died, and Mordecai adopted her as his own daughter. When Haman, the king's servant, came looking for a prospective queen to replace Vashti, he chose Esther from among many other women. There was a big feast held on Esther's behalf, but Haman and the king were not aware that Esther was Jewish, because Mordecai had instructed her not to tell anyone.

After Esther became queen, Mordecai won favor with the king when he discovered an assassination plot and reported it to the king through Esther. Based on the information from Mordecai, the conspirators were captured and hanged.

Haman, the king's right-hand man later became angry at Mordecai because Mordecai refused to bow down to him. Learning of Mordecai's ethnic background, Haman set out to have not only Mordecai destroyed, but all the other Jews as well. Haman convinced the king to go along with his plan.

All of the Jews were fasting and praying to protect themselves, and Mordecai told Esther to approach the king and beg for mercy for the Jews. The law, however, specifically forbade anyone to approach the king unless they had been summoned. To do so would bring a sentence of death.

Mordecai explained to Esther that if she did not approach the king, all the Jews would be killed. After receiving instructions from Mordecai, Esther prepared herself to approach the king, even though it was against the law. At the appointed time, Esther entered the inner courtyard of the palace. When the king saw her, he extended the golden scepter, allowing her to approach. Esther had the king's favor, and he was ready to grant any request she had. Esther requested that the king and Haman come to a royal banquet.

Later, the king honored Mordecai for having discovered the plot to assassinate the king. The tables were turned on Haman, who had thought the king was going to honor him. Esther invited the king and Haman to a banquet, where she revealed that Haman devised the plan to have the Jewish people destroyed. The king was so angered by this that he ordered Haman to be hanged on the same gallows that Haman had built to hang Mordecai. After this, the king granted Haman's estate to Esther, and she placed Mordecai in charge. Esther also asked the king to revoke everything bad that Haman had ordered for the Jews, and the king granted her request. New laws were written on behalf of the Jews. Again as Esther had requested and the king had ordered, Mordecai was promoted to a position in the kingdom second only to the king himself.

Esther's courage and her willingness to go before the king resulted in the freedom of her people. For such a time as this, Esther came to the palace and made a difference on behalf of her people.

Personal Point

It's safe to say that my time in San Francisco was short lived. Four weeks of training camp and my time was up. Looking back, there's no question it was the toughest training camp I had ever gone through. I can remember days when all I wanted to do was go home. But there was something in me that said, *Keep hanging in there.* But if I ever see Rocklin, California again, it will be too soon. Rocklin was the town where the 49ers held their camp and where my physical and mental anguish took place. Finally, when it was all over and the roster was complete, my name was not posted as one of the forty-seven players who would start the season in San Francisco. Instead, I was cut and let go with no sense of where I was going to go from here.

The following three days, my wife and I spent time planning our next move and closing out the businesses we had in the San Francisco area. My agent and I discussed whether there was any interest from any other teams. No one had yet contacted him, and all we could do was wait. Stephanie and I drove all the way from California to Detroit, where we lived during the off season.

During the course of those three long days of travel, it was as if God—who had seemed silent—was actually working behind the scenes on our behalf. When you truly begin to understand the character, mind, and heart of God, you realize that He hasn't forgotten what your prayers and requests are. He is actually working while you are waiting. It's similar to what happens in most churches across our country, or what happens when a ministry plans and prepares for an event. Or what happens during the week in preparation for Sunday games. We see the finished product, but so much has taken place behind the scenes for that finished product to look or perform the way it can.

As we continued our travels, Motel 6 became our place of rest and the local café was our choice of dining. And we enjoyed every bit of it. Shortly after we arrived in Detroit, my friend Byron called. He had seen on the news that I'd been cut by the 49ers, and he mentioned that the Carolina Panthers had released one of their running backs and needed someone to fill the spot. We both saw it as a good opportunity, but never really considered that God had worked it all out while we were driving back to Detroit.

The very next morning, guess who called me? You guessed it, the Carolina Panthers, inviting me to play with their team. I could not believe what had just taken place. Immediately, I called Byron back to share the good news with him. He was totally taken aback.

The next day, I was off to Carolina. The Panthers had no idea how much they were going to improve their running game. It took me a couple of weeks to learn their system, and I would get my chance, against the Tampa Bay Buccaneers, to show the organization that I was the piece they were looking for.

Twenty-seven carries and 124 yards later, not to mention a fifty-four-yard touchdown run, I had established myself as the Carolina Panthers' starting running back. And even though we were a brand new franchise, we won seven games that year. And even though I didn't join the team until opening day and didn't play until the third game, I rushed for nearly 1,000 yards that season. Had it not been for a knee injury, I might have finished the year with 1,500 yards and twelve touchdowns. What an incredible example of how God can do the impossible.

Only God can hold us together when we seem to be coming apart. But thanks be to God who gives us the victory through our Lord and Savior Jesus Christ. He not only makes a difference in our lives, He *is* the difference in our lives.

Inspirational Point

Sometimes, when it seems you're out of options and you don't know which way to turn, it turns out that God has been preparing you "for such a time as this." When you're facing doubt and uncertainty about the future, keep these three things in mind.

■ **1. Don't underestimate the impact you can have.** If you had told me that I was going to be a part of the expansion Carolina Panthers football team, miss the first two games of the season, and still run for almost 1000 yards, I would've said you had lost your mind. Had I been told at the beginning of the season that all that would happen, I wouldn't have believed it. A team that had not established a running game all of a sudden could run the football and do it with great success.

I guess I just didn't consider that the impact could be felt throughout the organization and would set the foundation for where the franchise was headed. So, please don't underestimate your impact in a situation. You will be amazed at what you bring to the table.

■ **2. Don't be surprised that you are doing what you're doing.** Sometimes with our acts of courage in a situation, or our success, we can amaze even ourselves—so much so that it can change the direction of our future.

Sometimes, all we can do is collect our thoughts and enjoy the moment. We often are our worst critics. We can fail to see in ourselves something that others have seen all along, a level of greatness and potential that God can use for His own glory in our lives.

■ **3. When you act, it creates a reputation that can be seen by others.** Who doesn't want to be known for some noble effort or some fantastic achievement? It's safe to say that most of us do. We enjoy getting some recognition for what we've done, especially if we've done something good. There's absolutely nothing wrong with a certain level of success. If anything, it's a testimony to others that we are utilizing our God-given gifts and are performing at an outstanding level. God is pleased when we use our position, our gifts, and our abilities to serve and honor Him.

Chapter 10

Confidence Is the Key
HOPE IN SOMEONE ELSE

Motivational Point

In order to succeed, you need to have confidence in yourself. A deep belief in oneself is an essential element in achieving anything. Without it you're just whistling Dixie. But I'm not talking about a confidence based on self-reliance. No, not the kind that's based on our own ability to get the job done. I'm talking about the kind of confidence that is placed in someone else, the full assurance, trust, or reliance that our lives are in the most capable hands around.

Let's consider a few propositions. First, in order to have the right kind of confidence in someone, there must be an established track record developed over a period of time, which demonstrates the person's reliability. Second, there must be an occasion where the person has demonstrated a unique ability to accomplish what it is you're seeking. Third, there must be evidence that the person has performed reliably on behalf of someone else. In some cases, you may be an eyewitness to it. As a result, you have full confidence that this person can and will deliver. As a short yardage specialist for the Detroit Lions, I knew that the one thing my teammates had full confidence in was my ability to pick up short yardage on third downs and to score in goal-line situations. I won their confidence by being placed in those situations over and over again and having repeated success. Rarely, if ever, did I fail. Okay, maybe once or twice. There was that one time against the Chicago Bears . . . but let's not talk about that.

Over time, I developed a track record with my teammates. They knew that if they could get the ball down to the goal line, they were going to score. Even when Barry Sanders came out of the game and I went in, and the defense knew right where the ball was going to go, they just could not defend it.

During one game against the Minnesota Vikings, in what was a tremendous game, we came down to the wire with a fourth-and-goal situation from the two-yard line. If we wanted to win the game we had to do it right now. One play. One chance. The 75,000 fans in the Metrodome in Minneapolis were as loud as any crowd I had ever heard in my life. The noise meter was at full tilt.

If the Vikings stopped us, they would win the game. If we scored, we'd win. The play was 35 Blast, and we lined up in what we called our "Heavy" set: five offensive linemen, two tight ends, a quarterback, two running backs, and a wide receiver. Lined up at the fullback position was Chris Spielman, our All-Pro linebacker. Chris weighed about 250 pounds and I weighed 230 (that's why they called it our Heavy set). The snap count was on first sound, because the longer you extended the snap and cadence, the more every offensive player had to hear. Any time it was as loud as it was that day in the Metrodome, you didn't waste time with long cadences. Therefore, the quarterback came up under the center and yelled, "Go!" And from the left side we went. A mass of humanity. Chaos everywhere.

Chris Spielman led the way, and I followed. When the whistle blew, I was securely in the end zone. We had scored and tied the game. The crowd that a minute ago had been so deafeningly loud was now absolutely silent. As I made my way back to our bench, everybody was congratulating the offense and telling me that they'd had no doubts that we were going to score. In their exact words, "We had full confidence that you were going to get it in the end zone." Our kicker trotted onto the field, kicked the extra point, and we won the game.

Is there anyone in your life in whom you have absolute confidence, believing that they can do for you what you need to have done? If not, then the person I recommend is Jesus Christ. You and I can have complete confidence that the Savior of the world can do exactly what you need Him to do. And He has already done one thing. He died on the cross for our sins and made it possible to know God the Father. Everything else is a piece of cake.

Spiritual Point: Daniel in the Lions' Den (Dan. 6:1–28)

It pleased Darius to appoint 120 satraps to rule throughout the kingdom, with three administrators over them, one of whom was Daniel. The satraps were made accountable to them so that the king might not suffer loss. Now Daniel so distinguished himself among the administrators and the satraps by his exceptional qualities that the king planned to set him over the whole kingdom. At this, the administrators and the satraps tried to find grounds for charges against Daniel in his conduct of government affairs, but they were unable to do so. They could find no corruption in him, because he was trustworthy and neither corrupt nor negligent. Finally these men said, "We will never find any basis for charges against this man Daniel unless it has something to do with the law of his God."

So the administrators and the satraps went as a group to the king and said: "O King Darius, live forever! The royal administrators, prefects, satraps, advisers and governors have all agreed that the king should issue an edict and enforce the decree that anyone who prays to any god or man during the next thirty days, except to you, O king, shall be thrown into the lions' den. Now, O king, issue the decree and put it in writing so that it cannot be altered—in accordance with the laws of the Medes and Persians, which cannot be repealed." So King Darius put the decree in writing.

Now when Daniel learned that the decree had been published, he went home to his upstairs room where the windows opened toward Jerusalem. Three times a day he got down on his knees and prayed, giving thanks to his God, just as he had done before. Then these men went as a group and found Daniel praying and asking God for help. So they went to the king and spoke to him about his royal decree: "Did you not publish a decree that during the next thirty days anyone who prays to any god or man except to you, O king, would be thrown into the lions' den?"

The king answered, "The decree stands—in accordance with the laws of the Medes and Persians, which cannot be repealed."

Then they said to the king, "Daniel, who is one of the exiles from Judah, pays no attention to you, O king, or to the decree you put in writing. He still prays three times a day." When the king heard this, he was greatly distressed; he was determined to rescue Daniel and made every effort until sundown to save him.

Then the men went as a group to the king and said to him, "Remember, O king, that according to the law of the Medes and Persians no decree or edict that the king issues can be changed."

So the king gave the order, and they brought Daniel and threw him into the lions' den. The king said to Daniel, "May your God, whom you serve continually, rescue you!"

A stone was brought and placed over the mouth of the den, and the king sealed it with his own signet ring and with the rings of his nobles, so that Daniel's situation might not be changed. Then the king returned to his palace and spent the night without eating and without any entertainment being brought to him. And he could not sleep.

At the first light of dawn, the king got up and hurried to the lions' den. When he came near the den, he called to Daniel in an anguished voice, "Daniel, servant of the living God, has your God, whom you serve continually, been able to rescue you from the lions?"

Daniel answered, "O king, live forever! My God sent his angel, and he shut the mouths of the lions. They have not hurt me, because I was found innocent in his sight. Nor have I ever done any wrong before you, O king."

The king was overjoyed and gave orders to lift Daniel out of the den. And when Daniel was lifted from the den, no wound was found on him, because he had trusted in his God.

At the king's command, the men who had falsely

accused Daniel were brought in and thrown into the lions' den, along with their wives and children. And before they reached the floor of the den, the lions over-powered them and crushed all their bones.

Then King Darius wrote to all the peoples, nations and men of every language throughout the land: "May you prosper greatly!

"I issue a decree that in every part of my kingdom people must fear and reverence the God of Daniel.

> "For he is the living God
> and he endures forever;
> his kingdom will not be destroyed,
> his dominion will never end.
> He rescues and he saves;
> he performs signs and wonders
> in the heavens and on the earth.
> He has rescued Daniel
> from the power of the lions."

So Daniel prospered during the reign of Darius and the reign of Cyrus the Persian.

Even as far back as the days of Daniel, there have been schemes and plots set against those who are upright and pleasing in the eyes of God. Daniel was a man who found incredible favor in the eyes of the Lord and also in the eyes of the king. Daniel was no doubt a man of integrity, who won the king's support due to his exceptional qualities.

The high officials chosen by King Darius found it disturbing and wrong that the king would select Daniel to be over all the king's other satraps and other administrators, so they plotted maliciously to destroy him. This is a classic case of what jealousy and envy can do. The other administrators could not deal with the fact that Daniel, a foreigner, was given authority over them.

Therefore, with a set purpose to destroy Daniel, they manipulated the king. Unable to accuse Daniel of anything against the law, they decided to create, with the king's approval, a new law prohibiting anyone from praying to anyone except for King Darius himself. If anyone was caught violating this edict within the next thirty days, he or she would be thrown into a lions' den.

Knowing full well that Daniel always prayed to God, the officials were prepared to catch him in the act.

Now is when the story gets interesting, because when Daniel hears about the new law, the first thing he does is go home to pray. He might have gone to the king and attempted to plead his case, but he didn't. Instead, he approached the King of kings and pleaded his case there. Three times a day, Daniel got down on his knees and prayed. And of course the administrators found him praying to God. When they took their news back to the king, Darius had no option but to carry out his decree.

"So the king gave the order, and they brought Daniel and threw him into the lions' den" (Dan. 6:16). A stone was set over the mouth of the den, and the king sealed it with the signet ring of his nobles. But now, look at this: then the king went home to his palace and spent the night fasting, and he was unable to sleep, because of Daniel's situation.

The next morning, the king ran quickly to the lions' den. He cried out in anguish for Daniel: "'Daniel, servant of the living God, has your God, whom you serve continually, been able to rescue you from the lions?'

"Daniel answered, 'O king, live forever! My God sent his angel, and he shut the mouths of the lions. They have not hurt me, because I was found innocent in his sight. Nor have I ever done any wrong before you, O king'" (Dan. 6:20–22).

Have you ever wondered if God is able to rescue you from your den of lions? Then wonder no more, because the same God who rescued Daniel from the lions' den can rescue you from your troubles as well.

Daniel had confidence in God. Do you have the same kind of confidence in God? Do you trust God to truly be able to rescue you from harm and danger? There is no greater person in whom to place your trust and confidence. You can have confidence in God. Daniel surely did.

Personal Point

It had been a long road, with many ups and downs, turns and twists. But my moment of truth had finally arrived. What I had felt I was capable of doing three years earlier, I was now on the verge of accomplishing—becoming a starting running back in the NFL. Looking back, it's amazing to think about what an accomplishment it really was. To put it in perspective, the NFL has thirty-two teams, which means that only thirty-two running backs can be starters. And now I was one of them. Only God could have made that possible. Then again, with God all things are possible.

To say that I was overjoyed would be an understatement. What was most incredible to me was all the unconventional circumstances God had used to bring me to this point: the transfers from one university to another; my showing in the all-star games, but still not getting an opportunity; my release by the Falcons after my second year; my time as a short-yardage specialist with the Lions; and being cut by the 49ers after training camp. Now that I think about it,

God used the worst of my circumstances to get me to the best of circumstances.

Of course, there was still one last hurdle. Because the Panthers didn't pick me up until right before the season started, I had to learn their system as quickly as I could.

It wasn't until the third game that I was able to establish myself as the starter. I'll never forget when coach Dom Capers called me into his office. Now let me tell you, for an NFL player, there's always an element of fear anytime you get called into the head coach's office—because oftentimes, it seems, the worst is about to happen. I kept my calm, however, and caught my breath.

With my nerves on edge, I could hardly believe what he told me.

"Derrick, congratulations," he said. "We as a staff have decided to make you our guy." I immediately left his office and went home to share the news with my wife. We both were amazed. Then we went to God in prayer to thank Him for the blessings in our lives.

Certainly I was nervous, but I knew that I hadn't made this possible. I was convinced that God was the One who had opened the door. And the same God in whom I had placed my confidence before, the same God who had brought me this far, was the same God I could place my confidence in again.

I knew that opportunities like this didn't come often, but I also knew that if I kept my confidence in God, then maybe one day I'd get my chance. Now here it was. In the inaugural season of the Carolina Panthers, I found myself on top of the football world. For the first time, I felt like I had finally arrived. Not only was I the starting running back for the Panthers, but I was now a part of history.

Because it was the first year of the franchise, everything

we accomplished was going to be a first. So, for example, however many yards I gained during the season would be the Panthers' rushing record. As it turned out, God had an even bigger surprise in store for me. Not only did I establish the rushing record for the Carolina Panthers in their first year, I set an expansion team rushing record that still stands to this day. And I accomplished that feat in spite of not playing in the first two games of the season, and missing six other games because of injury. No other running back in NFL history has rushed for more yards in the first year of an expansion team than I did in Carolina.

If you want to see the impossible happen, then don't place your confidence in anyone or anything less than Almighty God.

Inspirational Point

Who can really fathom what God is able to do on behalf of those who place their confidence in Him? Daniel had no doubt that God was reliable and trustworthy. Even though he was placed in a very difficult situation, Daniel still realized that trusting God was the key to his safety and success.

Do you see God as someone you can rely on? Do you have confidence based on a long-standing relationship with God? Or do you have confidence in God based on what He promised others who have believed in Him? Here are three points to ponder.

■ **1. Check out your past with God.** Confidence in God can come as a result of what you have experienced with God in the past. Has God ever done something in your life? Has He ever delivered you from anything? If so, then those experiences will fuel your confidence in Him as you go forward. Do you know anyone whom God has favored because of their trust in Him? If so, use that example as a confidence builder. I'm often impressed by the testimonies of other people who tell me what God has done on their behalf. I believe that if God can and will work on behalf of others, then certainly He can do the same for me.

■ **2. Check out your present with God.** Do you live your life in constant dependence on God for your daily provision? Is your confidence in God today? Confidence in God comes as a result of daily time spent with God. In those moments, you get a chance to see what God is like and how much He really cares for you. Then, when troubles come, as they are guaranteed to do, the daily time you've spent with God will give you the ability to trust Him completely.

■ **3. Check out your future with God.** The confidence we have in God is that He has secured the future for those who place their confidence in Him. No matter what happens in this life, God will always show up in some fashion to leave His mark on your situation. You can have confidence in the fact that He is a very present help in times of trouble. That's why so many characters in the Bible who found themselves in difficult places could have confidence beyond reason. You too can have this same confidence.

Chapter 11

Get Out of the Boat

PUTTING YOUR FAITH INTO ACTION

Motivational Point

If you're really reaching for the absolute best that God has for you, it's going to take you outside your comfort zone. It may even take you beyond your wildest imagination. If your *it* is going to happen, it may require the most illogical, bizarre, or radical thinking possible, the kind of thinking that causes others to shrug their shoulders and say, "That makes no sense at all! There's no way that can be done."

Have you ever been faced with an insurmountable task, that's only made worse by considering the most mind-boggling way in which to deal with it? The obvious won't suffice. It's going to take a heart that believes in God for the impossible. Can you see that it's not just you waiting on God to do something; it's also God waiting on you to do something?

Typically, the formula we hear for inviting God's intervention is "praying + waiting = our expected results."

Often that's true, but not always. Sometimes the formula is "praying + *not* waiting," because it's God who is waiting on us to step out in faith so He can demonstrate His power in our lives. What happens is that God acts as a support system in our faith decisions. When we step out into the unknown, God steps out and reveals the unknown and makes it known. It is God who makes the unfamiliar familiar.

I confess that I would much rather have God be the One who moves first, but that's not always the way He works. I love the scene in the movie *Indiana Jones and the Last Crusade* where Indiana Jones is about to take a huge step and cross a ravine. The problem is that there appears to be nothing to step on to support his weight. When he takes his first step in faith, however, the beam that couldn't be seen can now be seen, thus making it possible for him to walk across safely. You see, the victory is already there in most cases, we just have to believe it is. What makes us so hesitant is that the first step is the scariest step to take. But even though it's scary, it's also the most rewarding.

Some will suggest that every step forward starts with God. And they're right. Everything starts with God. Without the provisions that God makes on our behalf, nothing would be possible. But because God has promised to provide for all our needs, anything and everything is possible. God's first step is toward us. The Bible says, "For God so loved the world, that He gave His only begotten Son, that whoever believes in Him shall not perish, but have eternal life" (John 3:16 NASB). God has made forgiveness and acceptance possible through His Son, Jesus Christ.

God took the initiative, and now it's our turn. Steps are required if we are to experience the salvation promised by God through His Son. If we are to do the impossible, if we are to do the inconceivable, if we are to do the unthinkable, then it all starts with steps toward God. If you're ready to take the first step, don't worry. God has already taken the toughest step. You remember that one, don't you? The step that led Him to Calvary.

Spiritual Point: Peter Walks on Water (Matt. 14:22–33)

Jesus made the disciples get into the boat and go on ahead of him to the other side, while he dismissed the crowd. After he had dismissed them, he went up on a mountainside by himself to pray. When evening came, he was there alone, but the boat was already a considerable distance from land, buffeted by the waves because the wind was against it.

During the fourth watch of the night Jesus went out to them, walking on the lake. When the disciples saw him walking on the lake, they were terrified. "It's a ghost," they said, and cried out in fear.

But Jesus immediately said to them: "Take courage! It is I. Don't be afraid."

"Lord, if it's you," Peter replied, "tell me to come to you on the water."

"Come," he said.

Then Peter got down out of the boat, walked on the water and came toward Jesus. But when he saw the wind, he was afraid and, beginning to sink, cried out, "Lord, save me!"

Immediately Jesus reached out his hand and caught him. "You of little faith," he said, "why did you doubt?"

And when they climbed into the boat, the wind died down. Then those who were in the boat worshiped him, saying, "Truly you are the Son of God."

One of the greatest lessons in our relationship with Jesus is captured in these twelve verses, in which Peter learns the magnificence of Jesus' power (power, I might add, that isn't experienced apart from Peter stepping out of the boat). The moment Peter steps out of the boat, he experiences what Jesus is experiencing.

I love the fact that this story takes place early in the morning. It's good to know that Jesus works around the clock on our behalf. Even at a time when most people are sleeping, Jesus is working. In this case, the disciples happened to be awake. And the reason they were awake was because a storm was raging.

When Jesus came walking toward the boat on the sea, the disciples were terrified. In my years of ministry—speaking at retreats, conferences, and other church events—I've found that many people discover how afraid they are at the initial moment of giving their lives to Christ. Mostly, they are afraid of what lies ahead, of what God will do with them if they give their lives to Him by responding to His call. But in the moment of salvation, we don't approach God; He approaches us first. Therefore, it's the same situation the disciples faced when they saw Jesus walking on the water toward them.

The question is, what do we do with the fear that grips us after we've heard the call of God? In some cases that fear causes us to remain in our seats, which is what happened with the other disciples who were in the boat with Peter. I can't tell you how many times I have heard people say, "I really wanted to come down, but . . ."

What we must do is continue to focus in on the call, because with the call comes the comfort. Though the situation may be frightening, Jesus comforts us with the words, "Take courage. It is I. Don't be afraid" (Matt. 14:27). And the miraculous takes place.

When it comes to getting out of the boat, God knows we're all afraid. So He deals with our fear by reassuring us: "Don't be afraid." At the moment of decision, Peter still needed some assurances that it was indeed Jesus who was out there on the waves. So he says, "Lord, if it's you . . . tell me to come to you on the water." And Jesus says, "Come," allowing Peter to walk on water as He was doing (Matt. 14:28–29). When we step outside the relative safety of the boat, we experience the power of Jesus.

When someone comes forward to accept Jesus as Lord and Savior, they are truly coming as a result of the power of God. But here's the point: if you're going to walk on water and experience the abundant life, it can never happen unless you get out of the boat. You can hear the message a thousand times over, but if you don't come forward with your heart and receive Jesus, you can never walk on water. Satan's last chance to keep you from experiencing the abundant life happens when you're taking that first step over the side of the boat. Once you've stepped out in faith, the devil can't snatch you from the Savior's hand.

Of course, just because you've stepped out of the boat and you're walking on the water doesn't mean you're not surrounded by distractions. When Peter stepped out, he noticed the wind, became scared, and started to sink. Satan attempted his last effort to interrupt Peter's beliefs at this point. But thank God that the power to move forward rests in Jesus and not in us. When Peter started to sink, he cried out, "Lord, save me!"

What can be more genuine than an outcry for help? We are all sinking in the ocean of the world, but the Master of the ocean can calm the wind, steady our steps, and save us from the depths.

Personal Point

Who would've thought that I could have come so far, from being a kid who barely played high school football to starting in the NFL? Only God could have engineered something so incredible. On a cool and crisp autumn afternoon, the Carolina Panthers were playing the San Francisco 49ers. That's right. The same 49ers who had cut me loose just a few weeks earlier. The same 49ers who were defending Super Bowl champions, with players such as Jerry Rice, Steve Young, and John Taylor. Dom Capers, our coach, decided to make it a very special moment for me by naming me a team captain.

Our team really had its game face on, and we took it to the 49ers that day. Kerry Collins, our quarterback, threw the ball well. Our receivers, led by Willie Green, caught the ball really well. As the fourth quarter wound down, we were in absolute command with only two minutes remaining. We began what we called our victory offense, simply running down the clock. But then, on one of the final plays of the game, I injured my left knee and had to be carried off the field. It turned out that I had torn my medial collateral and posterior cruciate ligaments and part of my meniscus. I was terribly disappointed and knew my season was in jeopardy.

For me, the most difficult part of the injury was mental. Rehabbing my knee was definitely tough, and the time I spent away from the team was really tough. I hated not being able to compete. Fortunately, I was able to return for the last two games of the year. My first practice coming back was a test of my mental will. I knew I had been cleared to return by the doctors, but I still was a bit hesitant to go all out. I remember really looking to the Lord for help and comfort.

The weeks passed, and eventually I was ready to play again. As it happened, I made my return against the 49ers, the same team I had hurt my knee against. Because they were conference rivals, we played them twice a year. Coming back against the 49ers only accelerated my nervousness. The trainers gave me a knee brace so that I could regain my confidence, but I knew where my true confidence was placed. I could hear the Lord in my conscience saying, *Have courage.* And I knew I could walk on water. It was all the assurance I needed to go forward in faith.

With the power of the Lord helping me to run, I was able to experience great success against San Francisco. My knee was no concern, and once again the Lord demonstrated His presence in my life.

Are you in a place in your life where you need to step out of the boat and experience the power of God? Are you "coming back" from a hurtful or difficult situation? If so, God can be trusted to the extreme. Walking on water has never been a problem for Him. And it won't be a problem for you, either, if you'll just get out of the boat and take that first step toward Jesus.

Inspirational Point

Walking on water is never an easy assignment. As a matter of fact, it's an impossible thing to do. No one can really walk on water. Or can they? All I know is what I've read and what I've experienced in my own life through the person of the Holy Spirit.

The Bible says that Jesus walked on water and so did Peter. The point is that no circumstance is an impossible circumstance where Jesus is concerned. If He wants you to walk on water, you'll walk on water. Here are three points to reassure you.

■ **1. Know the heart of the One who told you to get out of the boat.** Who can comprehend the heart of God for those whom He created? And all the more so for those who have placed their faith in Him through the person of Jesus Christ. It says in John 3:16, "God so loved the world, that He gave His only begotten Son, that whoever believes in Him shall not perish, but have eternal life" (NASB).

God's only Son gave His life so that you and I would have life. His heart beats for you and will never stop.

■ **2. Keep your eyes on Jesus, no matter what.** Believe me, I know how tough this can be, particularly when we're tempted to look to other things. It's so easy to be concerned about the storm going on around us and lose our focus on Jesus. But the Bible encourages us in those moments. Hebrews 12:2 says, "Let us fix our eyes on Jesus, the author and perfecter of our faith."

No matter what the crisis or situation, the key to getting through it rests on our ability to trust God even when it appears that all hope is gone.

■ **3. Know that you're going to make it.** You don't have to know exactly *how* you're going to make it, but you do need to know *that* you're going to make it. Things may not turn out the way you expect, but you have to be able to see that your situation is going to end in your favor. It has to be that way, because that's what God has promised. God has said, "Never will I leave you; never will I forsake you." So we say with confidence, "The Lord is my helper; I will not be afraid. What can man do to me?" (Heb. 13:5–6).

Chapter 12

You Are Not Alone
GOD IS THERE

Motivational Point

Let's face it. It's very easy to believe you're on your own when it comes to the trials of life. No family member can truly understand. No friend can be found. And you have no idea when things are going to change. Have you ever been there, in that place where you feel as if nobody can possibly be in the same situation that you're in? Simply put, it's the place of pain and agony. But it's the perfect place to discover the presence of God. Do you not know that God hangs out in difficult spots? Really, since Adam and Eve, the whole world has found itself accustomed to being in places and involved in things that have made life a difficult ride. That's why I truly believe we find God to be such a present help in the time of trouble. Difficult circumstances are not unfamiliar grounds for the living God. He is totally used to dealing with us when things are really bad.

God has made it His divine appointment to be present in our moments of great dismay. After all, the Gospels capture countless stories of Jesus meeting people at their point of pain and providing a strong presence that can deliver them from their calamity. In difficult circumstances, do you know that Jesus can always be found nearby? And like the Lion of Judah that He is, He always is ready to pounce. God understands that, due to the fall of Adam and Eve, most of our lives will be spent dealing with problems. I still can hear my mom saying, "If it ain't one thing, it's another." If you look at the life of Jesus, you'll see He was always acting on behalf of someone, doing what they couldn't do for themselves.

Jesus seemed to have a certain attraction for difficult situations. Maybe that's because the very reason He came to earth was to help those who needed it most (which, by the way, includes all of us). He loves us so much that He promised to always be with us. He is with us even "to the very end of the age" (Matt. 28:20). If you truly know God and truly understand how He works, then you understand that He is constantly leading you. There is no place or situation that God has not led you into. It is always the case that God is doing a greater work in your life than your circumstances may indicate. He is constantly at work to make you into the person He wants you to be.

The Israelites were led away from Egypt by the hand of God, and they were led to the Red Sea by that same hand. When they reached the shores of the Red Sea and saw that the Egyptian army was hot on their heels, they became greatly concerned. But what appeared to be a dead-end situation, a body of water that was impossible to cross, was in fact only the prelude to God's miraculous provision for them. That's right, despite all appearances, God was right there in the middle of their situation. He wanted them to learn that if He was capable of leading them into it, He was also capable of leading them through it. And through it they went. And we all know the rest of the story: Pharaoh's army drowned in the Red Sea, and the people of Israel continued on their journey to the Promised Land. If you're following God, you can rest assured that no matter what the situation is, He has led you there for a purpose. And He is with you there, and will stay with you all the way. You can be certain of one thing: you are not alone.

Spiritual Point: Shadrach, Meshach, and Abednego in the Furnace (Dan. 3:8–30)

At this time some astrologers came forward and denounced the Jews. They said to King Nebuchadnezzar, "O king, live forever! You have issued a decree, O king, that everyone who hears the sound of the horn, flute, zither, lyre, harp, pipes and all kinds of music must fall down and worship the image of gold, and that whoever does not fall down and worship will be thrown into a blazing furnace. But there are some Jews whom you have set over the affairs of the province of Babylon— Shadrach, Meshach and Abednego—who pay no attention to you, O king. They neither serve your gods nor worship the image of gold you have set up."

Furious with rage, Nebuchadnezzar summoned Shadrach, Meshach and Abednego. So these men were brought before the king, and Nebuchadnezzar said to them, "Is it true, Shadrach, Meshach and Abednego, that you do not serve my gods or worship the image of gold I have set up? Now when you hear the sound of the horn, flute, zither, lyre, harp, pipes and all kinds of music, if you are ready to fall down and worship the image I made, very good. But if you do not worship it, you will be thrown immediately into a blazing furnace. Then what god will be able to rescue you from my hand?"

Shadrach, Meshach and Abednego replied to the king, "O Nebuchadnezzar, we do not need to defend ourselves before you in this matter. If we are thrown into the blazing furnace, the God we serve is able to save us from it, and he will rescue us from your hand, O king. But even if he does not, we want you to know, O king, that we will not serve your gods or worship the image of gold you have set up."

Then Nebuchadnezzar was furious with Shadrach, Meshach and Abednego, and his attitude toward them changed. He ordered the furnace heated seven times hotter than usual and commanded some of the strongest soldiers in his army to tie up Shadrach, Meshach and Abednego and throw them into the blazing furnace. So these men, wearing their robes, trousers, turbans and other clothes, were bound and thrown into the blazing furnace. The king's command was so urgent and the furnace so hot that the flames of the fire killed the soldiers who took up Shadrach, Meshach and Abednego, and these three men, firmly tied, fell into the blazing furnace.

Then King Nebuchadnezzar leaped to his feet in amazement and asked his advisers, "Weren't there three men that we tied up and threw into the fire?"

They replied, "Certainly, O king."

He said, "Look! I see four men walking around in the fire, unbound and unharmed, and the fourth looks like a son of the gods."

Nebuchadnezzar then approached the opening of the blazing furnace and shouted, "Shadrach, Meshach and Abednego, servants of the Most High God, come out! Come here!"

So Shadrach, Meshach and Abednego came out of the fire, and the satraps, prefects, governors and royal advisers crowded around them. They saw that the fire had not harmed their bodies, nor was a hair of their heads singed; their robes were not scorched, and there was no smell of fire on them.

Then Nebuchadnezzar said, "Praise be to the God of Shadrach, Meshach and Abednego, who has sent his angel and rescued his servants! They trusted in him and defied the king's command and were willing to give up their lives rather than serve or worship any god except their own God. Therefore I decree that the people of any nation or language who say anything against the God of Shadrach, Meshach and Abednego be cut into pieces and their houses be turned into piles of rubble, for no other god can save in this way."

Then the king promoted Shadrach, Meshach and Abednego in the province of Babylon.

I must confess that I have never experienced severe persecution because of my faith. There are people in the world, however, who have experienced great persecution. Even unto death they have stood and proclaimed the name of Jesus. That's the kind of young men that Shadrach, Meshach, and Abednego were. They dared to stand up for God, the only God they felt they had to worship, and they risked their lives to do so.

When Shadrach, Meshach, and Abednego refused to bow down and worship the statue set up by King Nebuchadnezzar, the king was furious and demanded to see the three young men. When they were brought to him, he said, "Is it true . . . that you do not serve my gods or worship the image of gold I have set up? . . . If you do not worship it, you will be thrown immediately into a blazing furnace. Then what god will be able to rescue you from my hand?" (Dan. 3:14–15).

I'm intrigued by how the three young men replied: "O Nebuchadnezzar, we do not need to defend ourselves before you in this matter. If we are thrown into the blazing furnace, the God we serve is able to save us from it, and he will rescue us from your hand, O king. But even if he does not, we want you to know, O king, that we will not serve your gods or worship the image of gold you have set up" (Dan 3:16–17).

Talk about confidence in God! In the face of the king's threats, they stood strongly and boldly for God. What a challenge for us to follow in their footsteps! What would we do if we were faced with such a level of persecution? It seems that Shadrach, Meshach, and Abednego never even thought twice about it.

The king then summoned his strongest men to carry the three young men to the furnace, which was heated to the highest temperature it had ever been. In fact, it was so hot that the soldiers who escorted Shadrach, Meshach, and Abednego were burned to death by the heat. You would think that would be the first sign that Almighty God was with the three young men, because they were not harmed. Not only that, but they soon had some company down in the furnace.

"King Nebuchadnezzar leaped to his feet in amazement and . . . said, 'Look! I see four men walking around in the fire, unbound and unharmed, and the fourth looks like a son of the gods'" (Dan. 14:24–25). The story goes on to confirm that Shadrach, Meshach, and Abednego were completely unharmed. Amen!

Is it possible to be rescued from such a plight as this? Is it possible for the angel of the Lord to encamp Himself around you, to keep you from harm and danger? Absolutely. He did it for the three Hebrew boys, and He can do it for you. Just remember: He can be found right in the middle of the blaze.

Personal Point

All along the way, I thought that being a starter—and, more importantly, getting a big salary—would be the defining moments of my career as a professional football player. But I soon learned that there's a lot more to being a pro player than getting a big contract. God had to have been in it from the beginning. I felt that I was following Him and He was leading me into all of these experiences. I discovered that He was truly right in the middle of all that was happening to me. It was no coincidence that I slipped from being a projected first- or second-rounder to being an eighth-round pick. It was no coincidence that I was dropped by the Falcons and picked up by the Lions. It was there that I met some of the godliest people around.

Most importantly, I met Dave Wilson. Dave is the team chaplain for the Lions. He really set for me a godly example of what Christianity was all about. He was an incredible spokesman for God's Word and a big inspiration in my life. God was completely in the midst of my circumstances. It was no coincidence that I ended up leaving Detroit and going to San Francisco, only to be released at the end of training camp. It was no coincidence that I was picked up by the Carolina Panthers and became the leading expansion-team rusher in NFL history. Neither was it a coincidence that I would be injured in the game against San Francisco, just after I was told by our general manager that I would be given a multiyear contract. It was also no coincidence that I would sign with the Arizona Cardinals the following season and finish my career much like I started it.

I can't help but wonder what would have happened if I hadn't gotten injured. Would I still have gone on to work with the ministry of Campus Outreach and disciple four young men who today are thriving in life representing Jesus Christ? Would I still have gone on to become the chaplain of the Georgia Tech athletic programs and have the opportunity to mentor and provide spiritual direction for young people who, without a doubt, will impact the world for Christ?

Countless other experiences from my playing days have left me with one conclusion: God was in the midst of everything, engineering and directing it as He chose so that He could be most glorified. He allowed me to pursue my dream, and yet He orchestrated my career so as to bring me to a place of total reliance on Him. And some of what seemed to be the worst breaks I could have encountered actually worked together for my ultimate good.

So, what are you pursuing? What is your dream, your *it*? I strongly suggest that you pursue God first and foremost. Surrender yourself to His will and His plan for your life. If you'll do that, then anything is possible.

It's possible. Especially when you follow the path of Jesus Christ.

Inspirational Point

When you decide to follow Jesus, isn't it great to know that you are following Him with a full understanding that wherever you end up, be it comfortable or uncomfortable, He led you there, and He is also there Himself? It's frightening to find yourself in places where God didn't lead you. Be certain that it is the God of the Bible you are following. Even when it feels as if you're all alone, realize that if God led you there, then He must be there Himself. To make it clearer, here are three points to remember.

■ **1. God is where you are.** Don't worry about being able to see Him. Sometimes you can and sometimes you can't. But what gives you your peace is not your ability to see Him, but your understanding of what He has promised.

As He says in Matthew 28:20, "Surely I am with you always, to the very end of the age." He has promised never to leave you or walk out on you. If He says He's going to be there, He will be there. You can bank on it.

■ **2. His presence will be felt.** One thing I enjoyed about the game of football was the fact that I always had a chance to make my presence felt in a game situation. Playing with Barry Sanders certainly taught me this lesson. The defense could stop him for more than three quarters of a game, but then suddenly they would make one tiny mistake, and Barry would be off to the races. When my turn came to play, I learned how to keep playing hard and to keep looking for the chance to make my presence felt on the field.

When God comes on the scene, you *know* He's there. You see, He's just too all-encompassing to be missed.

■ **3. His direction will be provided.** Don't ever concern yourself with what direction to take. Just ask God. You see, the way from here to there has already been mapped out for us in what I call God's road map for life. Yes, that wise old book called the Bible. If you will read it, it will get you from one place to the next with unbelievable care, wisdom, and power. Keep reading your road map. If you do, Heaven and your *it* are just around the corner. Happy travels, my friend. *It's possible.*

Conclusion

There you have it, a collection of life-changing events, moments, and principles that define how God showed up in various stories from the Bible, and how He acted on my behalf and revealed His presence and His plan for my life. Though the words of this book attempt to articulate God's involvement, they fail to adequately describe what it was like to actually be there, seeing the hand of God in each of those moments. There is something about feeling and experiencing the presence and the power of God that words cannot quite capture.

I guess I now know how the writers of those marvelous and God-inspired sixty-six books of the Bible must have felt: totally inadequate to communicate the stories of their lives. No wonder each and every letter was completely and totally inspired by God Himself. And I truly believe that if your *it* is burning in your soul to become a reality, then God is the way from where you are to where you want to be.

I'm not saying that the words of my book are God-inspired. But I am saying that He inspired me to write them for you. I hope each chapter has served as an inspiration to you. Bottom line, if your desires match God's desires for you, then look out!

My last nugget of advice is for you to stay on your knees in prayer. Why? Because the Lord wants to communicate a plan for your life—but you have to listen.

Stay inspired. In order to do this, I recommend that you grow consistently in God's Word. And don't ever give up. Believe in your heart that God can do anything except fail.

Finally, my prayer is that the message of this book will radically change the way in which you view God. I hope that my words and my personal story will give you motivation, inspiration, and the greatest gift of all—hope—to accomplish your *it* for God. Can I say with certainty that your *it* will happen? No, but if you embrace the twelve principles contained within these pages, you will accomplish great things for our risen Savior. Now go and make *it* possible.